AF316664

THE FOUNDER'S CREED

The Founder's Creed

Build Unshakable Belief
and Dominate Your Market

Patrick J. Sweeney II

ISBN: 979-8-218-88929-6 (Hardcover)
ISBN: 979-8-218-89293-7 (eBook)

Cover design by Patrick J. Sweeney II
Book interior design by Zoe Norvell
Printed in United States of America
For permissions: assistant@PJSweeney.com

To Beatrice

*Rowing alongside me as I swam across Duncan Lake was
an act of kindness that planted the seed for an amazing life.
You were the first person to believe in me.*

To Pat and Sandy

*Who told me I could be whoever I wanted
to be and do anything I wanted to do.*

Table of Contents

(continued)

INTERLUDE. FROM BELIEF TO BATTLE: THE INNER GAME — 95

PART II. THE LOOP OF CONQUEST (B.O.O.D.A.) — 105

PART I

FORGING YOUR CREED (THE 'B' IN BOODA)

1

The Belief Gap

On the morning of August 7, 1974, a slight man dressed in all black stepped into the sky. Philippe Petit placed one foot on a wire no wider than his thumb and walked away from the Southern Twin Tower in New York, as if gravity was a rumor. Thirteen hundred feet of emptiness opened beneath him. He had no net, no harness, no second chance—only the quiet Manhattan dawn and the six years he had spent preparing for this single moment.

Far below, New Yorkers froze on sidewalks, craning their necks, shading their eyes against the sun. Most thought they were witnessing the first stage of a suicide. But Petit wasn't courting death. He was practicing belief. He had tested every gust of wind between the towers, memorized every anchor point, studied every angle, sensed every tremor in the steel. To the crowd, it looked reckless. To him, it was inevitability. He wasn't defying risk—in his mind he had reduced risk to almost nothing through obsession, preparation, and conviction. He believed so completely in what he was doing that gravity itself seemed willing to negotiate on his terms.

When the police finally coaxed him off the other end of the wire at the North Tower, they asked, "Why did you do it?"

Petit gave a characteristically French shrug of one shoulder and explained, "There is no why. When I see a beautiful place to put my wire, I cannot resist."

To most people, that answer is madness. But to you, a founder, it's another Monday. Building a company isn't all that different from an epic tightrope walk. You've prepared. You've visualized. You've duct-taped together a prototype and a team. You've pitched it a thousand times in your head; in the shower, on your bike, lying in bed next to your spouse. And yet—when you finally launch, it still feels like you might have missed the wire and are in a free fall.

This book is about that moment—*before* your first step, and every uncertain moment after—when belief is your only safety net. The Founder's Creed will get you ready to blast through that uncertainty and set up a structure to make the right decisions in the shortest amount of time. You will learn to harness conviction and speed like lightening in a bottle.

Startups don't fail because founders are lazy or underprepared. They fail because doubt creeps in before conviction has a chance to harden. There's a space between the future you *envision* and what the world believes. I call it **The Belief Gap**. And your ability to cross it, and convince others to join you on that journey, determines whether you build a lifestyle business - or a unicorn.

To understand the potential lethality of poorly navigating this gap, look at one of the first Unicorns—Friendster. In 2003, they were a first-mover social network so dominant that Google tried to buy them...three times. They had the market, the technology, and the data. But as their systems began to crack under the weight of their own success, the leadership did exactly what thousands of founders do every day: they hesitated. They observed the pages loading slowly, and users complaining but they lacked a shared creed and the conviction to make a bold decision. Paralyzed by the fear of being wrong, they spent more time filing patents than fixing the product.

Meanwhile, a scrappy Harvard side project called "TheFacebook" was governed by a creed that valued *velocity* over perfection: "Move fast and break things." Mark Zuckerberg didn't necessarily have better data than Friendster; he had a tighter BOODA loop. He metabolized doubt into speed, while Friendster died in the hallways of wasted first-mover advantages because they couldn't decide fast enough.

Military strategists and Silicon Valley VCs will point you to a military doctrine called the OODA loop (Observe, Orient, Decide, Act) for speed in combat.

OODA works for fighter pilots. But for start-ups there is one crucial step missing from the loop—the one Friendster missed and Facebook mastered. **Before you can *Observe*, *Orient*, *Decide*, or *Act*...You have to *Believe*.**

This book is about that hidden force. It shows you how to create a personal creed that manufactures belief from scratch, makes it contagious, and turns Belief into your company's most powerful, scalable advantage. Because Belief isn't fluff. It's fuel. It takes planning, because without it nothing moves across the gap, and if you run out of it, like Friendster, you'll explode in a fireball of burning PR promises.

Figure 1—Philippe Petit crosses the Twin Towers August 7, 1974

Philippe Petit's walk was not a sudden impulse. It was the culmination of a six-and-a-half-year obsession, a meticulously planned operation he called "le coup." He and a small, ragtag team of co-conspirators studied the towers for years, forcing him to translate his private obsession into a shared mission—a wire walk of a spectacular kind, and the very challenge we will explore next. They forged fake IDs, disguised themselves as construction workers and architects, and smuggled hundreds of pounds of equipment to the rooftops. They had to solve logistics problems that made a NASA launch look like a paper route: how to shoot a cable over a 200-foot gap in a city that never sleeps. Then, how to anchor it down, how to compensate for the sway of the buildings and the wind shear at 1,368 feet, all while staying hidden from security guards.

Every step of the way, they were confronted by a world telling them their goal was impossible. Security personnel, engineers, the laws of physics, and the simple voice of common sense all screamed in unison: *you can't do it!*

The wall of doubt is where the real story lives. It's not about the 45 minutes on the wire. It's about the years spent in a state of unwavering belief while surrounded by a universe of disbelief. It's about the chasm that existed between the world inside Philippe Petit's head—a world where walking between the towers was not only possible, but destined—and the world outside, which saw only a madman with a death wish. Understanding belief is the key to dissecting the most audacious, world-changing, and often mystic figures in our society: Founders.

II.

Every year, hundreds of thousands of new businesses are started in the United States. They are launched from dorm rooms, garages, and coworking spaces. They are built on lines of code, on new recipes for gluten-free cookies, on pants that tighten up your tush or shirts that prop up your pecs, on robotic dog-walking apps and everything else under the sun (and Mars). And behind every single one of these businesses is a founder, or a team of founders, who have looked at the world as it is and have decided to build a piece of the world as it could be.

We have a standard narrative for these people. We call them visionaries, innovators, disruptors. We read about their brilliant ideas, their relentless "hustle," their uncanny ability to be in the right place at the right time and end up with nine-zero exits. Journalists look for someone leaving a dent in the world. Then we create a mythology around them, one filled with heroic tales of all-night coding sessions, ramen-noodle and Red Bull diets, and triumphant, flashy IPOs. The world of ordinary people loves that narrative. You know better.

You know, of course, that the story is dangerously incomplete. Praising a founder for his hustle is like trying to understand Philippe Petit's Twin Towers walk by obsessing over the brand of his balancing pole. You've admired the equipment and completely missed the terrifying, central fact of the matter: a human being is standing on a glorified clothesline a quarter-mile high in the sky, and the whole endeavor is insane.

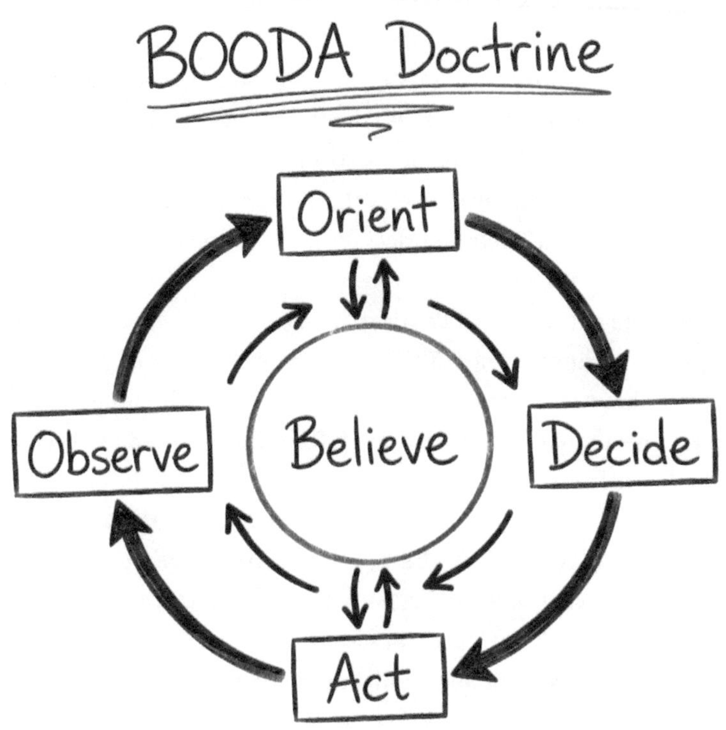

The battle-tested military doctrine you'll learn about is called the OODA loop (an acronym for Observe, Orient, Decide and Act). But the military gets to skip a step; Believe. Soldiers taste Belief in basic training every day, no one doubts the US military is the mightiest fighting force in the world. They issue Belief right along with the digital camo uniform and the bad haircut. You, as a founder, have to manufacture Belief from scratch, in a garage, or a spare bedroom, while being told you are crazy. That's the overlooked variable, the market inefficiency in every startup story. It's the 'B' that comes before everything else. First, you must Believe.

The most critical challenge a founder faces is not raising capital. It is not building a product. It is not finding the right domain name or leading a sales team. The most critical, painful, and fundamental challenge a founder faces is the management of the Belief Gap: This is the space between "This will never work" and "This will change everything."

It's the silence on the other end of the phone after you've just pitched your life's work to an investor who thinks you're confusing a hobby with a business. It's the polite, "This is interesting, but it's a little too early for us," which is VC speak for, "I don't believe a word you're saying, but I'm conflict-averse, so good-bye."

It's the look in your parents' eyes that mixes love with genuine concern for your financial and mental well-being. "A steady job has benefits, you know." They see the long hours, the mounting debt, the toll it's taking on you, and their protective instincts kick in. Their skepticism isn't malicious; it's born of love, which makes it even more potent.

It's the polite but vacant smiles of friends at a party who ask, "So, how's that little... website... thingy going?" They can't grasp the scale of your ambition, so they shrink it down to a size they can understand, a "little thingy," a hobby. The question isn't meant to be dismissive, but it feels like it is. It reminds you just how far your reality is from theirs.

It's the first employee who leaves, the guy who believed in you, who leaves for a stable job at a big company because he has a mortgage to pay and your dream is taking too long to cover his bills. This one cuts the deepest. It's not the skepticism of an outsider; it's the lapsed faith of a fellow believer. It's a vote of no confidence from inside the church. You're angry, then sad. Then doubt creeps in. I know I've lived it.

To be a founder is to live in a permanent state of cognitive dissonance, to hold two contradictory realities in your mind at once: the future you see clearly, and the present that offers scant evidence you're right. You have just enough validation to keep going—and enough doubt to keep you up at night.

Entrepreneurs already have a specific vocabulary for startup life—Minimum Viable Product (MVP), Customer Acquisition Cost (CAC), Total Addressable Market (TAM). We have frameworks and methodologies for everything from software development (Agile) to business model generation (The Lean Startup). **But we have no language, no framework, for the single most important resource a founder possesses: their own Belief.** And we have no way of measuring the toxic, corrosive effect that the Belief Gap can have on that resource.

The Belief Gap

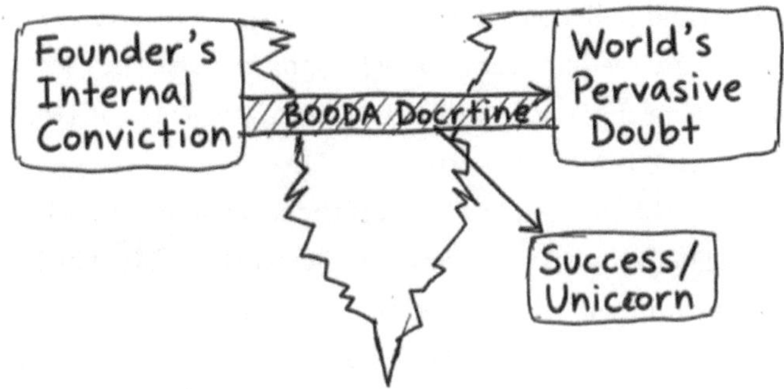

Figure 2—The Belief Gap requires founders to move internal and external supporters across together

You have to recognize the balance between knowing what you are selling is wanted in the market, versus, as my friend Mike Troiano (Boston-based VC) pointed out, the opposite; that fatal flaw which is an abundance of *unvalidated* belief. This is the condition Mike called the Belief Glut. That's basically a founder with an ego the size of Texas and a market that thinks you're selling pet rocks. You have no data that proves you're adding value to the world, just words and slides.

Founders have an abundance of confidence, but being in the Glut means you think you're early but in reality, you are blind. If you've been at it for a while and no clients are paying, no resources are using your solution, and you are the only one convinced that your idea could change the world; then you have an idealistic orientation to the market. If you're alone in your basement filling out obscure patent applications and no one is paying for your product; you're not building anything, you are stuck in the quicksand of a Belief Glut. It's an unrealistic view. It's your ego refusing to see reality.

The key to success, if you're a founder, is having product-market fit and knowing lots of people have the same problem you are fixing. What you need now is the launchpad, the foundation to manage that *growing* belief into something larger than life. That's when you start building an internal and external tribe of followers helping you build that bridge to hyper-growth. When you all follow the same creed, soon your idea grows out of being a start-up and starts to morph into a movement. If you build momentum; you build believers. When your believers become vested in your success you become more convinced you can deliver. This is how you overcome doubt. That's when you are crossing that Belief Gap with a team that is ready to blast off and a market that has validated you. That is when doubt diminishes and Belief blossoms. The snowball has started to roll downhill. The early acolytes are feeling a sense of belonging because they see what you see earlier than the rest of the world, earlier than ordinary people. It's that stage when the BOODA Doctrine is most powerful.

Think of it like this: a founder's Belief is the fuel (along with a healthy dose of Fear of course[1]). The business is the engine. The world is full of brilliant mechanics who can help you tune the engine, optimize its performance, and make it go faster. They will join you if they *believe* you're the right founder to lead them across the gap.

Paradoxically no one talks about the fuel. No one talks about how to refine it, how to keep the tank from running dry, or how to protect it from the water of doubt that seeps in from every direction. It's that doubt that creates the fear. It's the uncertainty and doubt that starts to run the tank dry. Most people just assume the tank is always full. It's not. And when the engine sputters and dies, we blame the mechanics or the design of the car. We rarely say, "Well, it looks like they just ran out of Belief." For all of us entrepreneurs who have lain awake in the middle of the night wondering if we would make payroll, we can feel it in our bones when the engine is running on empty.

III.

Can a small group of strangers have enough Belief fuel between them to save our planet from annihilation by aliens? In the late 1950s, the psychologist Leon Festinger infiltrated a small UFO cult in Chicago.[2] The group, led by a suburban housewife named Dorothy Martin, believed they were receiving messages from a superior alien race from the planet Clarion. The aliens, who called themselves the "Guardians," had warned of a great flood that would soon wipe out much of the United States. But the true believers, the members of the cult, would be saved.

---

1   *Fear is Fuel* by Patrick Sweeney hit #5 on the *Wall Street Journal* Best Seller List in 2020 and was the author's third book.

2   Leon Festinger, Henry Riecken, and Stanley Schachter, *When Prophecy Fails: A Social and Psychological Study of a Modern Group That Predicted the Destruction of the World* (New York: Harper-Torchbooks, 1956).

At the stroke of midnight on a specific date, a flying saucer would land in the backyard and whisk them away to safety.

Festinger and his colleagues wanted to know: what happens when a deeply held belief, a prophecy, is unequivocally disproven?

The believers took their preparations seriously. They quit their jobs, sold their possessions, and left their spouses (sounds like creating a start-up, doesn't it?). One member, a doctor, had spent years trying to develop a special kind of X-Ray machine; he abandoned his research and truly believed he would be beamed up to safety. It wasn't long when Dr. Festinger was told the night had come and they were going to get picked up. According to their plan, the group gathered in Martin's living room, waiting for their salvation. They had even removed all the metal from their clothing—zippers, bra straps, belt buckles—so as not to interfere with the delicate instruments of the flying saucer.

Midnight came. Nothing happened.

The clock ticked past 12:05. The silence grew heavy, almost physical. The disconfirmation was total and absolute. There was no flood. There was no saucer.

This is the moment of maximum pressure in the Belief Gap, it is the chasm of conviction.

The Belief Gap is the abyss between the founder's internal conviction—the Creed—and the external, contradictory evidence presented by the market. It is the distance between the world as you know it will be, and the world as it currently is. All founders have a Gap to cross in some form.

In the startup world, this moment happens every single day. It's the failed product launch. It's the demo that crashes in front of the big client. It's the moment when the world's skepticism seems to be proven right. You might think this is when people look at the reality and the rational response would be to abandon their belief. To say, "Well, we were wrong," and go home, zipperless and with loose, unclipped bras.

But that's not what happened in Chicago. They all stayed. Dismayed, but together.

At 4:45 a.m., Dorothy Martin's hand suddenly began to twitch. She grabbed a pencil and began to write, transcribing a new message from the Guardians. The message was ingenious. It explained that the little group of believers, by sitting there all night, had generated so much spiritual energy that they had single-handedly saved the world. Their belief stopped the flood. The aliens had not needed to rescue them because their faith had been a strong enough force.

Despair flipped instantly into euphoria. They weren't wrong; they were heroes! Their belief hadn't just been for their own salvation, but for the salvation of all mankind. Festinger's subsequent book, When Prophecy Fails, became a classic in social psychology, a manual for doubling down on crazy. Its central finding was a muddled paradox: for the truly committed, the disconfirmation of a belief does not destroy it. Instead, it can strengthen it, forcing the believer to reduce the dissonance by proselytizing even more voraciously like a madman. Before the failed prophecy, the group had been secretive and shunned publicity. Afterward, they were calling newspapers and trying to spread their message to anyone who would listen. They had to. The only way to lessen the sting of being wrong was to convince more people that they were right. And maybe they were...we'll never know.

This is a psychological phenomenon most of the world thinks is crazy but founders like you will know as the Belief Gap, or just another day at the office. A founder who has quit her job, invested her life savings, and convinced her family and friends that she is onto something big is not so different from the believers waiting for their flying saucer. The personal stakes are too high for simple disconfirmation to work. When a potential investor says, "I don't think there's a market for this," the founder doesn't hear a valid business critique. She hears a test of faith. An assertion to prove wrong. And like the cult members, her response is not to question the belief, but to double down on it. Those investors just don't get it yet, I'll show them.

This isn't as irrational as it may seem to the ordinary world. It's a part survival mechanism, part market insight. Without this almost superhuman ability to hold onto a belief in the face of contradictory evidence, no truly innovative company would ever get off the ground. Every great idea starts out looking like a bad idea. If it were obviously a good idea, someone else would have already done it. The founder's job is to protect that fragile, non-obvious idea from the world long enough for it to grow roots. They need to incubate the future inside their own mind first.

The goal of the founder is not to eliminate the Belief Gap, but to bridge it with irrefutable, market-validated data. Once they can convince someone to actually pay for their product or service, they are crossing that Gap with credible data, and those first one or two paid customers are the making of a big bridge across the chasm, turning a personal conviction into a collective, shared reality. The entire Founder's Creed is the blueprint for building that bridge.

IV.

Do you know the story of Brian Chesky and Joe Gebbia? In 2007, they were newly graduated artists from the Rhode Island School of Design, living in a San Francisco apartment they could barely afford. Their rising rent was far out pacing their pay raises and they were fighting to make monthly rent. They had a world-changing epiphany when an international design conference kicked off, and all the San Fran hotels were booked. Their idea: what if we threw a few air mattresses on the living room floor and rented them out to poor designers who needed a place to crash? They called it "Airbed & Breakfast."

They started with just three guests. It wasn't a business—just a clever way to cover rent. But in that awkward moment, something clicked. They had stumbled on a service people actually wanted. The question immediately emerged: what if this wasn't just a one-off? What if anyone, anywhere, could rent out a spare room? When you step back and imagine every empty room around the world—college kids heading off to school, roommates moving for a new job, guest rooms grand-parents only open at Christmas—it's a market not in the thousands, but millions. They realized if they could connect just a fraction of those rooms with users, they'd unleash a Mammoth.

They brought on a third co-founder, an engineer named Nathan Blecharczyk, to build the website and back end. Then they launched. And launched. And launched again. Each time, the result was the same: crickets. A handful of list-ings, a couple of bookings. The world was not beating a path to their door. It's at this point when our three founders were living deep inside the Belief Gap, and not seeing much of the other side. Their conviction was that they were creating a new category of travel, a global community built on trust. The world's response was, "You want me to sleep on a stranger's air mattress? Are you insane? That's how you meet serial killers."

The trio approached every venture capitalist they could find, dozens. They got a total of five meetings and zero interest. So they kept funding it themselves with Visa, and MasterCard, and Amex. By late 2008, they were broke and in debt. The prophecy seemed to be failing. The flying saucer wasn't coming. This was their midnight moment. But a different Cereal Killer saved the day, not the one the skeptical VCs were worried about.

The guys had a quirky, yet endearing, moment. They dreamed up an idea so far removed from their grand vision that it bordered on the absurd, but it showed their commitment to what they believed. It showed grit. The 2008 presidential election was in full swing. In a desperate, last-ditch effort to raise money, the two artists designed two limited-edition breakfast cereals: "Obama O's, the Breakfast of Change," and "Cap'n McCain's, a Maverick in Every Bite." They convinced a student at UC Berkeley to print 1,000 boxes of each. Then they spent days folding and gluing the boxes by hand and filling them with generic Cheerios and Cap'n Crunch. Once they had their supply, they packed up a van full of cereal and drove to the Democratic National Convention in Denver, Colorado. For an exhausting and highly profitable week they stood outside the Pepsi Center in downtown Denver hawking their breakfast cereal.

They sold them for $40 a box. They made over $30,000 in that week.

Think about that. The founders of a company that would one day be valued at over $100 billion, a company that would fundamentally reshape the global hospitality industry, were hand-gluing cereal boxes together to stay alive. They had the Belief that was strong enough to get them across the Gap no matter what it took. They had Observed that people who took advantage of their listings were really happy—they got a great deal, often in prime locations when hotels would have been two or three times more expensive. The product-market fit was real, not in their imagination. They just needed to learn how to get the word out and scale it.

This is life inside the Belief Gap. The story of the cereal boxes is often told as a funny anecdote about hustle and creative thinking. But it's much more profound than that. It was an act of dissonance reduction. Their core belief—that strangers could and should trust each other enough to share homes—was receiving miniscule validation from the market. So they found a different, smaller, crazier idea that could be used to fill up the Belief tank just a little more. People trusted these strangers enough to buy their cereal. Money came in. People are good and kind, and safe. It was a tiny, tangible proof point that they weren't entirely crazy. It was just enough Belief fuel to keep the engine from sputtering to a final, silent stop.

The investor Paul Graham, who would invite them into his famous accelerator - Y Combinator, later admitted he was baffled by the cereal story. He invested because of their Belief—he wanted to go from zero to one with these fanatics. He didn't invest in a good idea, he wrote a check for their unkillable spirit. "You guys are like cockroaches," he told them. "You just won't die." He wasn't investing in a business; he was backing their Belief.

We often look at Chesky and Gebbia gluing cereal boxes and call it 'hustle.' But that's a surface-level observation. If we could have slid Brian Chesky into an fMRI machine in late 2008 and scanned his brain, we would have seen something far more mechanical than 'grit.'

Modern neuroscience has identified a region called the ventromedial prefrontal cortex (vmPFC) as the brain's internal 'Value Accountant.'[3] Its job is to take incoming data—like five consecutive VC rejections—and decide how much those rejections should 'hurt.'

For most people, a 'No' triggers a drop in dopamine that shuts down creative problem-solving. But in the brain of a high-efficacy founder (like you) the vmPFC performs a radical calculation. It compares the 'No' to your internal Creed and labels the rejection as High Prediction Error.

The exciting science for founders is that the brain doesn't just 'overcome' the failure; it literally filters it out as noise. The cereal boxes weren't just a way to make rent; they were a biological reset. By selling one box, they gave their vmPFC a tiny, valid data point that 're-opened' the dopamine gate, keeping their brain's hardware running at 100% while their competitors' would have long since shut down from the stress of the 'Belief Gap. (To reset your own dopamine gate check out the exercise in the Founder's Creed Workbook available at www.thefounderscreed.com)

So what does the Belief Gap (or Glut) mean for you, the Maverick who wants to build something new? How do you navigate this gap without falling into delusion or despair or becoming consumed by doubt? The Founder's Creed isn't blind faith. It's not about ignoring reality. It's about managing the treacherous space between the world you see in your head and the world as it currently exists. It's about getting that core group to dive into that gap with you, and start moving as quickly as possible. That core group isn't just insiders, you need outsiders as well. There's a lot of uncertainty and that uncertainty is a big source of fear. In my best-selling book *Fear is Fuel*, I presented the neuroscience behind learning how to use fear as fuel. The Belief Gap is where you need that fuel most. Once you're comfortable with the uncertainty, it's time to courageously dive into the abyss, and when you do, you'll find others who want to dive in with you. The Founder's Creed will show you how belonging is contagious. Before you can move forward aggressively you need to position yourself with three quick actions.

---

3   Müller-Pinzler, L., Czekalla, N., Mayer, A. V., Stolz, D. S., Paulus, F. M., & Krach, S. (2022). Neurocomputational mechanisms of affected beliefs. *Communications Biology*, 5(1), 1241.

Step one is to name where you are. You have to acknowledge that the Belief Gap is real and you're crossing it. Rejection, isolation, doubt—these aren't signals that your idea is bad. They are the symptoms of trying to do something new. They are the weather patterns of the gap. When you can look at an investor's "no" and think, "Ah, this is that skepticism I was expecting," it loses much of its power. You can categorize it, analyze it, and move on, rather than letting it become a judgment on your self-worth.

Step two is to stop seeking validation and start finding belief partners. A co-founder, an early employee, a mentor, a spouse—someone whose most important job in the early days isn't the work they do, but the belief they hold. When your own belief is wavering, you can borrow some of theirs. The early Airbnb team wasn't just three guys building a website; they were a three-person belief-reinforcement loop. When two of them were ready to give up, the third would rally the troops. They were sharing the load of bridging the gap. Then to drive your team across the gap you need to get market validation—someone has to pay for what you do, even if it's reselling Cheerios.

Step three; learn the art of translation. Your belief is pure, uncut, and 200-proof. It's too potent for public consumption. You can't just walk into a banker's working capital committee and say, "I have a prophecy that this will change the world." You have to translate your belief into a language, or a story, the other side of the gap can understand. Translate your idea to market size, customer acquisition, and defensible moats. Build a bridge of data, however flimsy at first, across the chasm of doubt. What was most important for me in my five startups, is that I could translate techno-geek speak into concepts that a ten-year-old understands. It led to an industry defining book.

One of the best feats of marketing I ever did was write a book for the RFID industry when every Fortune 1000 company in the USA was trying to figure out the technology. But the key wasn't just writing any book, the key was writing RFID for Dummies[4] which has the highly prestigious title of the best-selling RFID book of all time (that means I beat out the other three). Why did that work as a marketing tool—because it made the technology easy to understand and used our methodologies and strategies as the de facto standards. It translated tech for the business leader. And it also gave my Dad a chance to tell all his

---

4	Patrick J. Sweeney II, RFID For Dummies (Hoboken, NJ: Wiley Publishing, Inc., 2005)

friends "He stuck with an audience he knows."

The cereal boxes were a form of translation. Chesky and Gebbia couldn't prove that people would welcome someone they'd never met into their home. But they could prove that perfect strangers would buy $40 boxes of cereal from someone they never met, and that people trusted each other. It was a flawed, almost comical translation, but it was better than nothing. It was a tangible artifact from the world of their belief that they could show to the world of skeptics. You won't find this insight about belief anywhere because most founders have had to discover it on their own.

This is the work. It's not just about building a product; it's about building the bridge of evidence, piece by piece, that entices others to cross the Belief Gap and join you on the other side. The first customer is a plank. The first dollar of revenue is a nail. The first positive review is a cable. Your job is to be the chief engineer of this belief bridge, obsessively collecting and assembling these small, tangible proofs.

Which brings us back to Philippe Petit and his cable across the Twin Towers.

When he stepped out onto that wire, he wasn't just taking a risk. He was making a statement. He was demonstrating, in the most dramatic way imaginable, the power of a belief to reshape the physical world. For six and a half years, the idea of a man walking between the towers was a fantasy, a private delusion. But for 45 minutes on that August morning, it became real. He forced the entire city of New York to inhabit his vision. He crossed the Belief Gap.

But here is the final, most important lesson. Petit didn't just scurry across the wire to get to the other side. He performed on it. He lived on it. He made the gap itself his home.

The Founder's Creed isn't about escaping the Belief Gap; it's about mastering it. Because inside gap is where resiliency grows, creativity sharpens, and conviction hardens. If your dream is living and breathing then you learn to dance on the wire bridging that gap, but first you've got to figure out where you are in the Gap vs Glut spectrum (The BOODA Doctrine workbook at www.thefounderscreed.com walks you through exactly where you are on the spectrum).

2

The Map of Minds

I.

After two years of macaroni and cheese dinners, "borrowed" bandwidth and solving most problems with duct tape, I thought opening a $25 million data center fortress meant we'd finally made it. What it actually meant was I built a very expensive stage for our team to act out the **illusion of agreement.**

ServerVault lived up to its name. It looked like something out of a Mission Impossible movie: touch-sensitive fences, Faraday walls, armed guards, inside always chilled to a perfect sixty-five degrees, a constant hum of processors, LEDs blinking like Morse code, racks of servers standing at attention. To get to our conference room, you scanned your retina and walked through vaults protected by former Navy SEALs.

It was a long way from where I started ServerVault. Our first "data center" was a single rack in a rundown 700 square foot office, pieced together with used Cisco and Sun gear and a T-1 line we'd "borrowed" from the neighbor's data center— technically with permission, but not exactly legal. Fast forward 18 months, and here we were, in Northern Virginia, next to AOL, the world's largest internet company, sitting inside a $25 million fortress under a giant banner that declared our mission in bold letters: Secure the Internet.

We believed it. Everyone around the table had staked their careers, reputations, and savings on that phrase. When I first told my vision to our CTO, he said with complete belief, "I can build that." And he did. Customers were signing up. Investors had written checks. From my chair at the head of the table, as the founder, it felt like alignment—one company, one mission, one team. We were crossing the Gap.

Belief is the entrepreneur's most powerful fuel, but it's also a dangerous drug. That morning, I realized we'd been high on our own supply. Somewhere between the mission banner and the biometric mantrap, I'd missed the obvious truth: we weren't aligned at all. We were building four different companies trapped in the same badass building.

JB, our rock-star CTO, was sketching a digital citadel on the whiteboard—moats of cryptography, battlements of firewalls, sentries of intrusion detection. For him, perfection was the network product, and he was ten years ahead of the rest of the industry.

Laudy, our COO, didn't see a fortress; he saw a factory. He wanted an assembly line that could add thousands of servers a month, update firmware automatically— use compute like a utility, scaled like a power grid.

Sue, our VP of Sales, wasn't interested in moats or grids or pings. She was already picturing her next client call. Her pitch was simple: fire your IT staff, save money, ServerVault will do it better. She wanted custom promises, attractive SLAs and immediate delivery dates. But those were SLAs JB wouldn't risk and dates Laudy wouldn't back.

Jimbo, our CFO, looked at all three like a man watching a controlled burn edging closer to his house. JB's fortress? Too expensive. Laudy's factory? Too complex. Sue's promises? Too...promissory. He saw a tidal wave of CapEx and fundraising rounds big enough to buy small countries. His concern hit home and was scariest of all because I always looked to him as the voice of reason. He was our adult supervision. It was clear to me then that the misalignment was burning capital and creating negative velocity.

Me and four leaders. One mission. Four different realities.

The banner said Secure the Internet, but each of us had our own translation. JB's vision made Laudy's impossible; Laudy's efficiency clashed with Sue's customization; Jimbo's spreadsheets vetoed everything. We weren't aligned—we were orthogonal.

The only way out of this illusion of agreement was to make the invisible visible. Put every belief on the table, side by side, and see where they overlapped and where they collided. That exercise became the prototype for what I now call the Shared Belief Map (SBM)—a tool that forces a team to draw a hard line between what we know, what we believe, and what we're just assuming. The SBM isn't a static whiteboard drawing; it's a refinery. Raw intuition flows in from the Memory, gets tested in the heat of the Engine Room, and only the irrefutable truth makes it into the Bedrock.

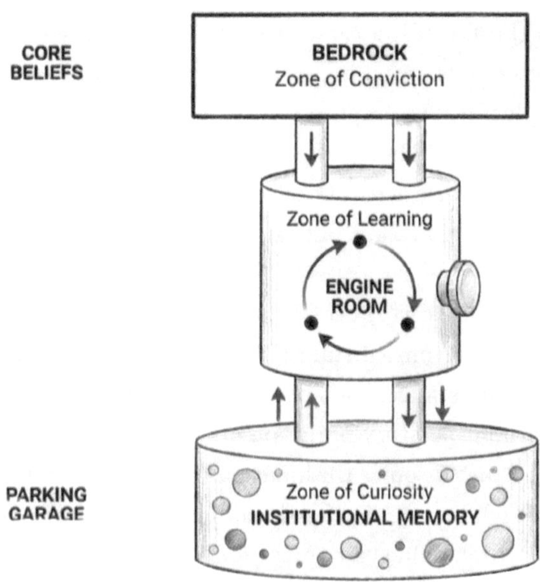

Figure 3—The SBM creates a Refinery for Beliefs.

Once we agreed on what we believed at ServerVault, the fog lifted. The vault, the factory, the sales pitch, the cash flow—they weren't wrong. They were incomplete. Plus our beliefs were focused in different directions. And until we had one shared map, we weren't running one company. We were just five smart people rowing in circles.

That experience of disconnectedness in the ServerVault data center wasn't unique to us. It's a scene that plays out in boardrooms and Slack channels every day. Brilliant, passionate people use the same words—"revolutionize," "dominate," "win"—while holding private, conflicting definitions of what those words actually mean in practice. They might have the Belief but it's not fueling the same outcomes. What if you interviewed the leaders in your company? Ask them what the top three priorities are and how the team should execute on those priorities. Would you get several different answers? Try it.

The focus and energy of Belief that shoots out in different directions is one of the silent killers of promising companies that have shown a product-market demand. It's the reason your rocket ship of a vision is still stuck on the launchpad, burning through cash and time idling away while the engine just makes noise, and the astronauts wait for their queue. Your job is to corral all the energy from belief in one direction strongly enough for lift-off.

Everyone on the founding team is passionate. Everyone is committed. Everyone uses the same big words: "We're going to revolutionize the industry." "We're building a platform to empower users." "We're changing the world one heated toilet seat at a time." Then you even convince venture capitalists or angels to go along on the adventure across the Belief Gap so they throw money into the Gap with you. This buys you time, but can also fund diversion, distraction, and mis-aligned priorities.

The problem is the PowerPoint deck and words like revolutionize and empower are just clouds. From a distance, they look like solid shapes, but up close, they're mist with no substance. Each person on the team has their own private, nuanced, and often contradictory definition of what those visions mean. The brilliant engineer hears "revolutionize the industry" and thinks of an elegant, scalable, technically perfect architecture. The savvy salesperson hears the same phrase and thinks of a specific, high-value customer segment they can personify and then close in the next quarter. The visionary CEO hears it and thinks of a ten-year plan for global domination.

Think about how often you see people speaking up or challenging you (or others on the founding team). At your all-hands meeting does everyone nod in agreement? Is their private understanding the shared understanding among everyone? They are all looking at the same cloud and seeing a different animal shape but thinking everyone sees the same three-toed sloth. This is the Illusion of Agreement. And it is at the heart of what eventually unravels the Belief in a company and helps feed doubt.

To see this play out in the most start-up-dense square mile in the world, let's go visit an exciting start-up in the Cambridge Innovation Center at One Broadway in Cambridge Mass—the heart of Kendall Square and MIT's campus, the Silicon

Valley of the East. We will call this start-up MedXit to conceal the details and founders. The company was founded by three rising stars: Dr. Sandra Rossi, a seasoned Mass General cardiologist; Giovanni Bianchi, a data-driven Harvard MBA; and Shannon Dunn, a brilliant full-stack engineer from MIT. Together, they aimed to tackle a problem each of them had felt personally in one way or another.

Their mission—"To empower longer health-span through accessible data and monitoring"—was bold and inspiring. With a $500,000 seed round from Boston-based friends and family, they leased sleek office space in the start-up hub called the Cambridge Innovation Center or CIC—the birthplace of many East Coast Unicorns. With a handful of good coffee shops and restaurants right next to the Kendall Square T-stop[1], they were fueled by espresso, conviction, and a sense of unstoppable momentum.

What was pulling them toward a slow death was that they weren't aligned. Not really. To me, the advisor brought in by their lead investor, it seemed like another ServerVault moment. Incredible talent, early product-market adoption but leaders rowing in different directions. This costs them a huge decision burden every day. Because every time you have to choose, and weigh out different options, you pay a price. We have a decision tax on our brains. That's why people like Steve Jobs (black mock turtleneck) and Mark Zuckerberg (grey hoodie) embraced daily uniforms. Not aesthetics, efficiency. Every decision you don't have to make frees glucose, oxygen and willpower for the choices that matter.

Sandra saw MedXit as a clinical tool built for physicians—rigorous, validated, and capable of saving lives. To her, credibility was non-negotiable. If it wasn't medically trusted, it wasn't worth building. Giovanni envisioned a sleek consumer platform—gamified, friendly, and fast to market. He wanted growth, virality, and user delight. Clinical trials could wait. Shannon, the engineer, just wanted to build something great; fast, secure, frictionless with AI. But with the other two founders pulling in a different directions, she was stuck designing a product that satisfied no one. The result? A feature-bloated, confusing experience that pleased neither doctors nor patients.

The tension was slowly growing each day. The Illusion of Agreement was pulling them into the heart of the Belief Gap in three different ways. On the surface, everything looked aligned. They had a mission statement, early funding, and

---

[1]   The "T" is what Massachusetts' Mass Transit Authority (MTA), or the subway, is referred to by locals.

promising technology. But beneath that, three separate worldviews were grinding against each other. They weren't just debating product features. They were interpreting reality through different lenses, and the company only had enough resources to focus on winning through one lens. So they decided to reset.

On July 24th, 2025, the MedXit team gathered in their Kendall Square office for a two-day intervention with me and one of their board members—a workshop to build their own Shared Belief Map (SBM). It was designed to take all their conflicting visions and distill them into a single source of truth. The setup was deceptively simple: lots of coffee, a bunch of muffins and Brioches from their favorite café—Flour Bakery - and the tools of titans to-be: a huge whiteboard, sticky notes, and a promise of brutal honesty. Each founder wrote down their key beliefs about customers, product, market, and regulation—then labeled them either a Core Belief or a Hypothesis. A Core Belief was truth, a Hypothesis needed to be proven or disproven. And that's when it happened.

Sandra placed a card that read, "Physicians must trust us as a certified tool to use in clinical care" - that's a Core Belief. Giovanni placed one that read, "Busy professionals will pay for real-time insights even if they aren't clinically validated." He called that a Core Belief.

They couldn't both be right.

That visible contradiction was a turning point. It forced the team to confront what they *thought* they agreed on—and where their beliefs actually diverged. They began reclassifying assumptions. Some were downgraded from Core Beliefs to Hypotheses. Others were discarded entirely. Some were put in the Garage for later testing.

It was awkward. It was uncomfortable. But it was clarifying. Now, with their Beliefs surfaced and sorted, they could finally begin to Observe.

Right now, you need to learn how to build that Shared Belief Map for your company—it's the single best tool you can adopt to get the collective energy of your company moving in the same, unambiguous direction (there is much more detail on holding a workshop in the BOODA Doctrine Workbook as well. Find it at www.thefounderscreed.com).

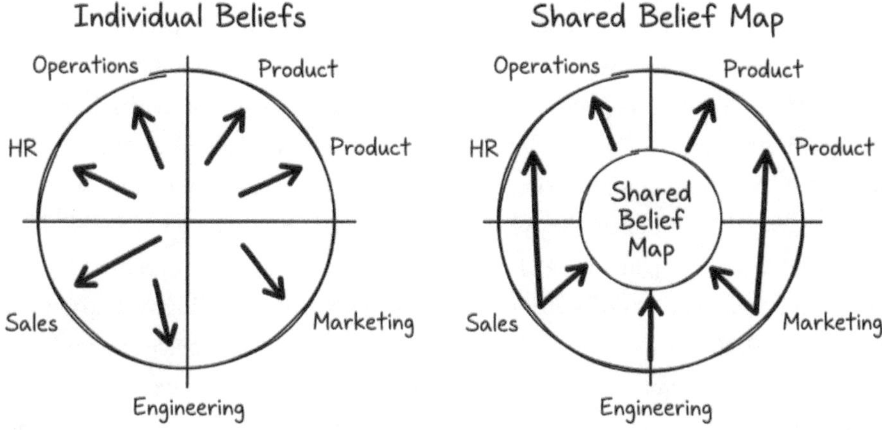

Figure 4—The Shared Belief Map gets the company moving in one clear, explicit direction.

II.

How do you fight an enemy you can't see? How can you put a spotlight on a wound that everyone is pretending doesn't exist? How do you stop a team of brilliant, passionate people from tearing their own engine apart?

In Chapter 1, I introduced the idea that a founder's Belief is the fuel for their startup, that and real product-market fit validation. A single founder with a full tank of high-octane Belief can go remarkably far on their own, or they can be lost in a Belief Glut. However, assuming you've got some validation, the moment a team forms and needs to run full speed ahead, supplying that high-octane fuel gets complicated. Of course, everyone is bringing their gas can, or bottle, to the garage. For MedXit, Sandra, the doctor, is showing up with a can of stable, long-burning diesel—her belief in clinical validation. Gio, the business guy, arrives with a canister of high-octane race car fuel—his belief in explosive, direct-to-consumer growth. Shannon, the engineer, just wants to build the most reliable engine possible, she's got stable unleaded 95 octane, but she's being told to design a system that can somehow run on diesel, unleaded and race fuel all at the same time. The result is an engine that sputters, knocks, and backfires. The team isn't moving forward; they're just burning fuel to create friction, noise, and smoke.

The problem isn't a lack of belief. The problem is a lack of *shared* Belief. The fuel isn't being refined or cleaned and certainly isn't ready to power anything.

What they needed was a refinery (See figure 3). They had a process to take all their individual, crude beliefs, pour them into one place, and distill them into a single, high-grade fuel source that the entire engine is designed to run on. They used that tool to make their private beliefs public, to debate them, and to decide, together, what kind of fuel they will be. That's their Shared Belief Map (SBM).

The SBM is not a business plan. A business plan is a glossy brochure for out-siders, showing pictures of a promised land and maybe some slideware to get you there. The SBM is the GPS coordinates on a map—it's the one place you and your team are trying to get to. It's a messy, honest, and powerful process for insiders. Its purpose is not to project confidence, but to create it. It forces the uncomfort-able conversations needed to turn a collection of individual passions into a single, focused, and formidable force. Even with founders who have been together for a while and share an overlapping belief I have seen the SBM transform struggling startups into hyper-growth near-Unicorns.

The SBM has three main sections, each designed to refine the fuel in a dif-ferent way.

1. **The Bedrock (Mission, Vision, and Values):** This is the high-level distillation. It sets the destination and the rules of the road. The Mission is the North Star, the "why" that never changes. For example, at my first startup, ServerVault our mission was "To Secure the Internet." Big, bold, and audacious. Philippe Petit our rope walker, famously said "there is no why." But he clearly had a mission of turning the unimaginable into a stage for beauty and awe. Your Vision, broken down into 1, 3, and 10-year horizons, forces the team to agree on the specific landmarks they'll pass on the journey. This means one, or two main priorities, not ten. The Values are the behavioral guardrails, the non-negotiables that keep the car on the road and the Creed clear to everyone.

2. **The Engine Room (Core Beliefs vs. Hypotheses):** This is where the real heat and pressure are applied. It's where the crude oil of assumption is siphoned into its most valuable components. By forcing the team to distinguish between unshakable Core Beliefs and testable Hypotheses, it separates the Bedrock from the sand. It creates a shared belief and

agreement that can make the most efficient use of their fuel.

3. **The Parking Garage (The Institutional Memory):** This is the crucial overflow tank. It's the designated space for every important thought, question, or tangential ideas that emerge during the process. The Garage keeps your culture from becoming rigid and monochromatic because you have a source for future hypothesis.

This is the work. It's not about finding a magic formula. It's about building a machine that turns disagreement into alignment, and alignment into fuel. This is your structure for hyper-growth.

The heart of the Shared Belief Map is Core Beliefs and Hypotheses. It's a simple table where the team must list their 5-7 most critical assumptions about their world. But here's the twist: for each assumption, you must tag it as either a Core Belief or a Hypothesis.

The distinction between Core Belief and Hypothesis is everything you just saw with MedXit.

A Core Belief is a truism. It is a foundational assumption that you are treating as a fact. You are betting the entire company on this being true, and you don't doubt it. You do not spend time or money trying to validate a Core Belief. All your energy is focused on *acting* upon it. A Core Belief is a statement of faith. It's your "We hold these truths to be self-evident." For example if the Massachusetts Department of Health and Human Services pledged funding so that "300,000 citizens will be on remote telehealth and monitoring by 2027" that could be a Core Belief that needs no testing or validation for MedXit. It's a fact.

A Hypothesis, on the other hand, is a data point that's *questionable*. It is something you *suspect* is true, but you don't know for sure. Every Hypothesis is an opportunity to learn, to change perspective, and to get ahead of your competitors. A Hypothesis must be testable, falsifiable, and most importantly (as you'll see later) observing this Hypothesis is a job assigned to a single owner. The owner's job is to design an experiment or test to get an answer. That answer may trigger the use of the kill switch we'll explain later in the chapter. In our MedXit world, saying that they will have 20% market share (60,000 clients) by 2027 is a Hypothesis that needs to be constantly evaluated.

Let's go back inside the MedXit workshop. In the small conference room were the three founders and one of their investors (whose "white hair" of experience helped him go from just an investor to the only outside board member) excitedly mapping out their future. I asked the team to silently write down their key beliefs on sticky notes, covering five areas: Customer, Product, Market, Operations and the Legal/Regulatory landscape. Their entries followed a simple format:

Area	Describe the Belief or Hypothesis	Tag	Owner (if Hypothesis)
Customer	Our customers (doctors) will only trust our product if it's backed by peer-reviewed clinical trials.	Core Belief	
Customer	Our customers (busy professionals) will pay for our product if it saves them time and gives them actionable health tips, regardless of clinical validation.	Core Belief	

Sandra, the doctor, writes: "Our customers (doctors) will only trust our product if it's backed by peer-reviewed clinical trials." She walks up to the whiteboard and places the sticky note in the "Customer" row. I ask, "Core Belief or Hypothesis?" "Core Belief," Sandra says, without hesitation. "This is non-negotiable. It's the foundation of my medical ethics."

Next, Giovanni walks up. He places his sticky note in the same row. It reads: "Our customers (busy professionals) will pay for our product if it saves them time and gives them actionable health tips, regardless of clinical validation." I ask the same question. "Core Belief," Gio says firmly. "Our entire business model depends on a low-friction, direct-to-consumer approach. We can't wait years for clinical trials."

And there it is. The Illusion of Agreement is shattered. The hidden conflict is now visible to everyone in the room, stark and undeniable.

The company cannot simultaneously bet its existence on two mutually exclusive truths, and in fact if you asked three different people, you'd get three different answers, so they aren't really truths. This is the ultimate example of a Hypothesis. There needs to be more data to prove it as a Core Belief. Hypotheses are not facts, they have not been proven. Both Sandra and Gio got it wrong. This is their "Aha" moment.

The room goes quiet. This is the time of truth. The conversation that follows is painful but productive. Eventually, they reach a compromise. Sandra's belief is too fundamental to her identity and to the long-term credibility of the brand, but it doesn't mean it has to be true for the company to succeed. Similarly, if Giovanni is not correct the company can still prosper in other ways. However, with a Core Belief, a fact, a change in that could devastate the future of the company. A great Core Belief for MedXit is that the Massachusetts government has committed to paying up to a Billion dollars for its citizens to get telehealth in the next five years. That is a fact, and therefore a Core Belief. Giovanni and Sandra both agree to classify their beliefs as Hypotheses and will try to prove them right over the coming weeks and months.

The new sticky note reads: "We *hypothesize* that we can acquire an initial user base of 1,000 'beta testers' by offering them a simplified version of the product while we pursue full clinical validation."

So the correct SBM entry looks like this:

Area	Belief or Hypothesis	Tag	Owner
Customer	Acquire 1,000 non-medical Beta testers	Hypothesis	Gio

Do you see the power of this simple change?

The conflict is transformed into a plan. It's no longer Gio's belief versus Sandra's belief. It is now the *company's* shared mission. And the Hypothesis has a clear goal (1,000 users) and a clear owner. Giovanni is assigned the task of designing and running an experiment to test the theory. His energy is no longer spent fighting an internal battle against Sandra; it's channeled into a focused effort to find the truth.

They continue this process for other areas and come up with clear answers:

- **Product:** Is "Our product must be accurate enough for a doctor to make a diagnostic decision" a Core Belief or a Hypothesis?
- **Market:** Is "Hospitals will pay a six-figure license fee for our platform" a Core Belief or a Hypothesis?
- **Regulatory:** Is "We can operate for two years without FDA approval by marketing ourselves as a 'wellness' device" a Core Belief or a Hypothesis?

Each question forces a debate. Each debate forces a choice. Each choice creates alignment. By the end of the day, their whiteboard is no longer a collection of vague aspirations. It is a clear, honest, and actionable map of their shared reality. It shows them the solid ground they all agree on (their Core Beliefs) and the treacherous terrain they must explore together (their Hypotheses).

III.

A map is only useful if you check it regularly on the journey, after all how many times have you blown by a turn because you weren't watching the GPS, or you were absorbed in a Podcast? The Shared Belief Map is not a one-time workshop artifact that gets filed away and forgotten. It is a living document. It should be the home screen for the company's internal dashboard. It should be reviewed at every all-hands meeting and every board meeting because it focuses your Belief.

The primary function of the SBM is to guide the allocation of the company's most precious resource: time. **If an activity is not directly executing on a Core Belief or testing a key Hypothesis, the immediate question should be: why are we doing it?** The SBM becomes a filter for distraction and a lens for focus. That makes it a catalyst for speed and speed wins.

When Giovanni's experiment to acquire 1,000 beta testers succeeds, the map is updated. The hypothesis is validated. This gives the team confidence to invest more resources in that direction. If it fails, they don't see it as a failure. They see it as learning. The Hypothesis was wrong. They update the map, cross it out, and ask, "What is our new Hypothesis?" They can look in the Garage for things that may have been close to becoming part of the Map but didn't make the core focus the first time. This process creates a culture that is resilient, adaptable, and relentlessly focused on finding the truth. And it happens every single day.

This is where the Shared Belief Map reveals its true power: it is a tool for accelerating a team's metabolism. It allows a group of people to learn and adapt at a speed that is impossible for misaligned organizations to match. This is how you win. To understand this, we need to look at one of the most successful strategic doctrines of the last century, born not in a boardroom, but in the cockpit of a fighter jet.

The doctrine is called the OODA loop, a concept developed by the legendary Air Force fighter pilot John Boyd (I highly recommend his biography, simply titled *Boyd* by Robert Coram). Boyd wanted to understand why and how great pilots consistently won dogfights, even when flying technologically inferior aircraft. First, he created a key theory called the Energy Maneuverability Theory. Then he decided to put the ideas to work in a doctrine called the OODA loop. The pilot who could execute this loop faster than their opponent would win, every time. They could get "inside" their opponent's decision cycle, making the foe react to a world that no longer existed.

Most people haven't heard of the OODA loop, but its influence is everywhere, from military planning to business strategy. The US Airforce Adopted it as the primary way to engage the enemy. Then the Marines and Special Forces implemented it for ground combat and created an entire Doctrine for the Marines called Maneuver Warfare. In the business world, the CEO of JPMorgan, Jamie Dimon says they use the OODA loop constantly as a "strategic process of constant review, analysis, decision making, and action."[2]

But there is a problem with the OODA loop.

At its heart is a critical assumption that is often overlooked. The OODA loop works for fighter pilots because the most

Figure 5—Belief is already instilled in military uses of the OODA Loop. The US pilots never doubt they are the best.

---

2   2023 JPMorgan Letter to Shareholders, https://www.jpmorganchase.com/ir/annual-report/2023/ar-ceo-letters

difficult part—*believing* they can win and execute the OODA cycle—is already guaranteed for them before they ever leave the ground. A United States fighter pilot already has a deeply ingrained, shared belief system that the military aviators in the USA are simply the best in the world. That is not a Hypothesis, it is a Core Belief they all hold without exception. They believe in their training. They believe in the superiority of their aircraft. They believe their instruments are telling them the truth. They believe their wingman has their back. They believe they've flown more combat readiness drills than any other fighting force in the world. They don't have to debate the nature of reality while pulling 9 Gs. Their Belief Gap has been crossed. This unwavering Belief allows them to focus all their mental energy on Observing, Orienting, Deciding, and Acting. **The military was so successful with the OODA loop because they already had the B, but it has been silent, invisible, until now.** Ordinary people miss that key component of applying the OODA loop. You as a founder can see it clearly now that The Founder's Creed has shed light on the reality. Believe is your first step.

Let's go back to our team at MedXit before their workshop. They were permanently stuck in the fright of the first three phases—BOO (Believe, Observe, and Orient). Every decision was a new debate about the fundamental nature of their reality. Who believed what? What observations were they talking about and how should they orient against that data? Sandra would *Observe* a new clinical study, *Orient* herself in a world of doctors and patient safety, and *believe* that they needed to build a more rigorous validation feature. Giovanni would *Observe* a competitor's new feature, *Orient* himself in a world of consumer tech and market share, and *believe* they needed to build a seamless social login. They were running in place at BOO and not taking action! They were canceling each other out and not making collective decisions. Their cumulative speed was zero, maybe even negative.

The Shared Belief Map is a tool for getting a startup team out of the B phase that the miliary doesn't have to worry about. By making Beliefs explicit—by separating the bedrock of Core Beliefs from the shifting sands of Hypotheses—it gives the entire team a single, shared reality that guides their actions. It aligns their BOODA loops and that creates speed and executional hygiene.

When the SBM is in place, the team can finally move together. They *Observe* a point of market feedback. They can instantly *Orient* it against their maps: does this challenge a Core Belief or does it give us more data on a Hypothesis? They can then *Decide* on a course of action and *Act* on it, as one. The SBM allows a team of mavericks and visionaries to achieve the same precise execution as a squadron of Blue Angels pilots. It closes the internal Belief Gap so the team can turn its full attention to the external one of constantly accelerating through the loop to hyper-growth before your competitors.

The SBM also serves as a powerful tool for bridging that individual Belief Gap we discussed in Chapter 1. When an investor tells the MedXit team, "I don't think doctors will ever use a tool like this," they don't crumble. They can point to their map. "We understand your skepticism," they can say. "That's why 'Doctor adoption' is one of our key Hypotheses. Here's the experiment we're running to test it, here are the early results, and here's what we're learning. We investigate this every week in our BOODA stand-ups."

They are no longer defending a fragile, personal belief. They are presenting a rigorous, shared process of discovery. They are inviting the investor to look at their map, rather than just listen to their prophecy.

This is the ultimate purpose of this book, The Founder's Creed. It's not about having a perfect, unshakable belief from day one. It's about giving you the right tools to build and refine your Belief over time, first within yourself, and then within your team, then with the outside world. It will get you to the right focus, faster than anyone in your industry if you commit to a weekly rhythm and stick to your fundamental principles. It's the perfect fit for a company that had enough market traction to adopt a system like the Entrepreneurs Operating System but now is ready to hit the accelerator and scale at hyper-growth well beyond just a lifestyle business.

The most important thing you will ever build is not your product. It's not your company. It's the shared understanding that allows the product and the company to exist. To the rest of the world it may look like the future—but because of your Belief you are living in the future right now. The Vision of what that looks like is your fuel. Believe.

You've felt how speed is born—aligning that quantum power of Belief to be pointed in the right direction by everyone crossing that Belief Gap with you. Before we race into culture and indoctrination, there's one question you are likely still pondering: "Where am I on the Belief Gap–Glut spectrum today?"

Are you living in the healthy founder's gap (good), closing it (great), or stuck on an island of conviction with no one else crossing the bridge (dangerous)? There's a simple way to tell.

Here's what two very different companies looked like as they navigated the Belief Gap:

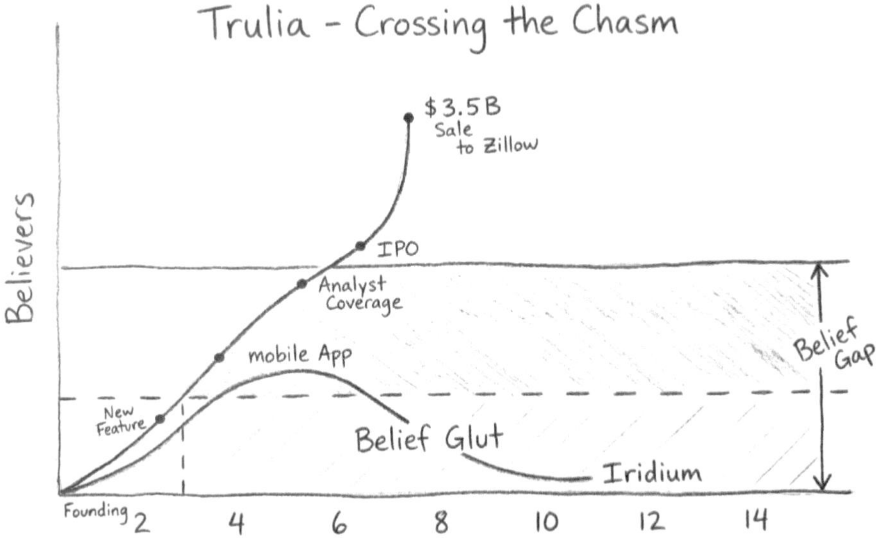

Figure 6—The Belief Gap and Glut illustrated by two very different companies.

Now you can self-score your company (3 minute exercise): Rate two categories each 1-10, where 1 is for very low Belief and 10 is absolutely no doubt and the strongest conviction. The best way to think of this is Believers over Time, so if you have two employees, then five, then 15 you are growing Internal Belief over time (how much time is critical). Then do the same for external—how many customers, how many Beta users, what are analysts saying, how about technology partners?

- **Internal Belief** — How many employees, investors, and advisors do you have supporting your vision? Do you share an unshakable, explicit mission; can you state your contrarian thesis in one sentence?
- **External Belief** — Customers/Analysts/Competitors/Jounralists are people beginning to echo your language; do new hires join for the mission; and most importantly, each quarter, is the pipeline getting bigger?

- **Interpretation:**

High Internal + Low External = **Belief Gap** (good—now build the bridge).
High Internal + ~Zero External = **Belief Glut** (island—confront reality & test).
Low Internal = **Weak Core** (fix belief before you scale).

IV.

You've done the self-score. The results are in. High internal belief, near-zero external belief. Welcome to the Belief Glut.

This is, without question, the most dangerous place a founder can live. It's the comfortable, fog-filled island of isolated conviction. The coffee is great, the pitch decks are beautiful, and you are surrounded by a teammate or two who all agree. The proverbial "Yes man (or woman)" while you are burning cash and going nowhere. If your "Belief" is just a delusion, does the BOODA loop just become a high-octane accelerant to drive you off a cliff? The answer is yes. It absolutely can. I know, because it happened to me.

This protocol isn't a theoretical exercise. It's the scar tissue from my most recent and painful failure: a company called DaVinci 3.0.

It all started on the muddy banks of the Charles River on a raw October Saturday at the Head of the Charles regatta. It was 2017 and one of the Winklevoss twins was holding court in a conversation with a group of maybe 10 of us in the US Rowing Association tent, protected from the frigid weather outside. I don't remember which twin it was, but I do remember how adamant he was about the future of Bitcoin and suggested we all get into it. Bitcoin was trading around $4,500 a coin. I didn't act then (although I should have) but I did start to investigate it and notice articles and posts online. By the following spring I had bought some BTC and was thinking about the next logical step for me. You've heard about my data center innovations at ServerVault and my early data center work with Trammel Crow. Bitcoin was mined in data centers, and I knew a lot of people in the industry who owned data centers. In 2020 I bought a couple of mining machines and started mining Bitcoin. I bought the leading brand, Chinese-made Antminer. It was loud and hot. It had a fan on one end of a shoe-box sized computer to push air over the 200 or so ASIC chips inside and another fan on the other end to pull out the hot air. Soon enough I started asking for space in some of my friend's data centers. It was about this time when Bitcoin mining was starting to be singled out for its negative impact on the environment. The inefficient design of the Antminer was an electricity hog. There were estimates that the US mining industry was using as much electricity as the entire country of Norway.

My daughter, Shannon, and I have always been particularly active in protecting the climate especially the fragile glaciers in the Alps - the massive seas of ancient frozen history that are slowly dying. When she and I were talking about Bitcoin around the dinner table one night she asked me with incredulity "You're not *mining* Bitcoin, are you Dad?" And like many people in the mining industry, I was making good money despite the inefficiency. But she was right—BTC was going to change the world, but at what cost if we kept doing the same terrible mining power by fossil fuels? That's when she challenged me—why don't you figure out a better way. That's when I called my friend Bruce at MIT who was a chip designer and systems engineer and told him I wanted to take a system design approach to solving the bitcoin energy issue. We were solving a problem of heat and waste. For every dollar of crypto you earned, you were spending a significant chunk just to stop the ASIC chips from melting.

The industry's solution was brute force: more fans, bigger fans, colder air. But my background was in building massive, ultra-secure data centers like ServerVault. Bruce and my other early engineers had taught, or were still teaching, their approach at MIT. This wasn't a hardware problem; it was a *systems design* problem.

The solution, I believed, was elegant. Instead of two fans, a controller, and a power supply for *every single miner*, what if you treated it like a high-performance engine? What if you submerged hundreds of mining boards into a single, custom-designed bath of immersion cooling fluid, all run by just one or two controllers? Way more efficient, much less maintenance, nearly zero water used, and 80% less electronic waste during the annual upgrade cycle—the perfect solution to a big problem.

It was efficient. It was modular. It was, I believed, a world-changing idea. We called it DaVinci 3.0 to give a nod to Leonardo and 3.0 for Web 3.0. It was sure to be a winner. I put the first half a million dollars of my own money in to test the idea.

We had the highest possible score on the "Internal Belief" metric. Our team was brilliant. Our conviction was absolute. Our "External Belief" score? We had interest. We had "atta-boys" from the mining community, particularly justified by an early investment from a publicly traded mining company. I cashed in a bunch of stocks and put more money in and we hired a contract manufacturing company to help us get to production. But we had zero, not one, paid contract, and were on the edge of a perfect storm.

We were living, in absolute, beautiful isolation, on the island of the Belief Glut.

We were honestly convinced we were onto something world-changing. A system-designed, environmentally friendly, more efficient way to mine Bitcoin. Home-run, I thought, and because the engineering was elegant, we assumed the business case would be solid. That's a trap of the Belief Glut: you think beauty equals truth.

Then came the sentence.

It arrived casually — not from an investor, not even from one of my engineers — but from a potential customer who was doing their own diligence. They had run our pitch up their internal flagpole and someone in their technical team noticed a single line in Antminer's warranty document and quickly said "No thanks."

"The warranty is void if the ASIC chips are submerged in immersion fluid."

One sentence. Twenty words. The entire foundation of our "revolutionary" system dissolved in front of my eyes.

Everything we had built — every dollar burned on prototypes, every late night debugging fluid leak issues, every design iteration Bruce and the MIT team had pushed through — was built on top of a component we didn't control, and a manufacturer rule we had somehow never seen. A business model with a built-in landmine.

I stared at that line like it was written in a different language. I blinked a few times, half-expecting the words to rearrange themselves into something less catastrophic. They didn't. That warranty language had been there from day one — the equivalent of a neon DO NOT ENTER sign we had somehow walked right past.

This wasn't an engineering failure. It was a failure of Orientation, and it was the first cloud of the storm starting to rip the hinges off the house.

We never asked the most basic question: What does the supplier require for this to work?

We were so convinced of our own genius — the cooling design, the sustainability angle, the modularity — that we skipped the unglamorous part of building a business: checking for fatal constraints.

This is why the Glut is so dangerous. You can have brilliant people, flawless logic, world-class engineers... and still miss the detail that kills you. We didn't just miss the market.

We missed the fine print. And the fine print always wins.

I didn't have the complete BOODA doctrine, at least not in its final form. I was running on pure, uncut "B" (Belief). The Belief (for a slightly arrogant, multiple successful founder- me) was blocking out the Observation and Orientation that I should have been doing—because I raised money from friends and family and put in another million of my own. We kept shelling right back out to contract manufacturers and chip designers. I even paid $40,000 to have a bunch of fake ASIC boards built so we could show off our design at a trade show—where we paid around $100,000 to fill a booth. I also thought that, like my old acquaintance Mike Saylor from Microstrategy, that putting most of our treasury cash into Bitcoin was a good idea. And when you're running that fast, you don't see the black swan event until its wings are already blotting out the sun.

The black swan's name was Sam Bankman-Fried. And he not only ripped the hinges of our house but took the entire frame right off the foundation.

When the FTX empire collapsed, it didn't just crash the price of crypto; it evaporated our entire market. The large miners we were talking to weren't buying new tech; they were filing for bankruptcy. That chunk of our own "cash on hand," our treasury that was in crypto vanished overnight.

We tried to pivot. We were smart. We saw the rise of AI. "Our immersion tech is perfect for hot, powerful GPUs!" we said. But we were reacting, not re-orienting. We were a solution looking for a new problem. The market saw us as "experimental." Investors saw us as "a failed crypto play." We were f*cked.

I had to learn this lesson the hard way. I put in a couple of million dollars of my own money trying to keep it alive. I lost it all. I lost all of my investors' money. DaVinci 3.0 died, slowly and painfully, on the island of the Belief Glut.

That failure is the "why" behind this next section. When you are in the Glut, the purpose of the BOODA loop is not to accelerate. It is to validate. The Doctrine is not a weapon to conquer; it is a navigation system to find out if you are hallucinating. It provides the off-ramp I wish to God I'd had.

If your score from above is "Belief Glut," this is your new, temporary operating system.

First, reframe your Shared Belief Map—and make everything a hypothesis to be proven. In the Glut, you have no proven "Core Beliefs." You have *only* Hypotheses. At DaVinci, our "Core Belief" was that miners wanted efficiency, and that Bitcoin mining was very profitable. That was wrong. It was a Hypothesis, and its default status was "unproven."

Second, install pre-determined Kill switches. A Hypothesis without a "Kill Switch" is just a wish. A Kill Switch is the non-negotiable, pre-committed off-ramp you need to keep from burning through millions. It's the point at which you *must* stop and Re-Orient. The Kill Switch has two parts; a Time-Bound Action: For example, you could start by validating the market and say "We will *act* by calling 50 target customers in the next three weeks to gauge interest." And second a Falsifiable Metric like "If we get *zero* paid pilots / *zero* letters of intent / *less than 1%* conversion, in three months then this hypothesis is invalidated."

Figure 7—Knowing when to hit the Kill Switch is a matter of life and death for a startup.

At DaVinci, our Kill Switch should have been: "If we don't have three paid-in-full contracts by the end of the quarter, this hypothesis is invalid. We stop." Hitting a Kill Switch is not a failure. It is a successful execution of the BOODA loop. It's using the data to Observe and Act and doing it quickly, so it keeps you from a $2 million lesson.

When in the Glut, the "Act" step is different. It is not about scaling at hyper-speed. The *only* goal of an "Act" is to get one, single, validating data point from a stranger who doesn't owe you anything. When you are running the BOODA Doctrine in hyper-growth validated space a normal "Act" means you are busy building the factory. However, when you're not experiencing hyper-growth and you're stuck in the Glut-Phase, then that means "Act" means you've got to pre-sell *one* ticket to the factory tour before you start laying the concrete. At DaVinci 3.0 Our "Act" was building the elegant system that worked well. Our "Act" *should* have been selling *one* system before we dumped millions of dollars into building the second system.

When I look back on some of the success factors that created lasting value in my career, I see the dynamic team at ServerVault as a great example. As the founder, you are the Chief Believer. This makes you biased. I know, I was an Old Faithful Geyser of Belief, spewing benefits and vision. Just keep in mind that if you are also that guy, then your job is to appoint a "Chief Skeptic." In my case it was Mr. Grumbles, my CFO at ServerVault and co-founder that would have no problem calling bullshit on some of my ideas. Your Skeptic's job is not to be negative. Their job is to own the Kill Switches. They are responsible for presenting the unvarnished data from the "Observe" phase of the BOODA loop and having the power to pull the plug.

This protocol is the antidote to delusion. It is the system that separates the visionary from the person stranded on the island. The Glut is a temporary starting point, not a permanent address. The BOODA Doctrine is your ticket off the Island.

3

The Speed of Belief

For a week, the MedXit office felt less like a startup and more like the victory lap. The Shared Belief Map, printed on a sheet of paper so large it looked like an architectural blueprint, hung on the main wall like a treaty signed after a long revolutionary war, a declaration of all they believed in. The air, once thick with the unspoken tension of three brilliant people rowing in different directions, was now light. They had a map. They had alignment. They had refined their individual passions into a single, high-grade fuel, and the engine was finally humming.

No one felt the hum more than Giovanni Bianchi. As the newly anointed owner for the "Beta Tester Acquisition" hypothesis, the map wasn't just a document to him; it was a license to hunt. He drafted a landing page, pouring his belief in aggressive, direct-to-consumer growth into a single, explosive headline: "Add three years to your life in 30 days." To Gio, this wasn't a medical claim; it was an A/B test waiting to happen. He had a piece of bait designed to see what the market would bite. It was only an opportunity for new data.

He walked toward Dr. Sandra Rossi's desk with the casual confidence of a man about to do a mic check before a big concert. He was expecting a quick thumbs-up. He got a five-alarm fire instead.

"Absolutely not," Sandra said, her voice quiet but carrying the clipped, final authority of a surgeon over an open heart. "This is medically unsubstantiated. It makes us sound like snake-oil salesmen."

"Sandra, it's a wellness app, in beta, not a medical journal."

The friendly hum of the office suddenly sounded like a high-voltage buzz. "We're not publishing in *The Lancet*. We need attention. This is how the game is played."

"This is not a game," she said, finally looking up from her monitor, her eyes communicating a principle Gio's spreadsheet couldn't quantify. "Our brand's credibility is the only asset we have. That headline shreds it."

And just like that, the victory lap was over. The alignment they had celebrated a few days earlier was revealed to be an illusion of a different kind. They had a map that told them *what* to Believe. They had just discovered, with the force of a canon fired, that they had no shared understanding of *how* to act. The map on the wall told them where to go, but it didn't tell them how to drive there. If you think of driving as constantly making a series of decisions—how much accelerator, when to stop braking, where to go into the curve - you soon realize even driving is a never-ending theater of choices. Choices can tire you out and drive you to slow, bad results.

II.

The most chilling demonstration of decision fatigue came not from a Silicon Valley founder, but from Israeli courtrooms. In 2011, researchers analyzed 1,100 parole rulings by eight experienced judges.[1] Crime? Background? Time served? All factors that mattered—just not as much as the time since their last snack. At the start of each session, parole approvals hovered near 65%. They sank steadily toward zero before the next snack break, then approvals shot back up after a bite to eat. In the graph below the X-axis isn't clock time; it is *cases since last calories*. When the judges were "hangry," they defaulted to the status quo: No. Say yes and you must open a new loop, justify a risk. Say no and the world stays the same.

---

1   Danziger, S., Levav, J., & Avnaim-Pesso, L. (2011). Extraneous factors in judicial decisions. Proceedings of the National Academy of Sciences, 108(17), 6889-6892

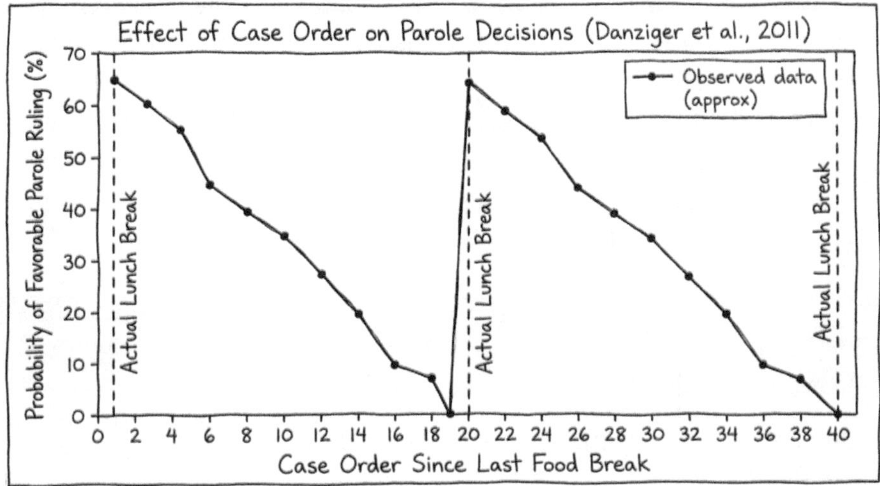

Figure 8—The time since the last snack was the largest determinate in a prisoner's chance of parole (2011—Danziger et al).

The MedXit team was living in their own courtroom every day after their strategy session. They knew where they wanted to go, so why were they spending so much time arguing and analyzing? Feature debate, headline argument, next-hire discussion—each withdrawal was emptying their cognitive bank. Without a clear operating system, they were constantly relegated to the same questions: speed vs. quality? data vs. intuition? employee vs. customer vs. investor? The decision tax compounds; the work slows; "no" wins by inertia.

That's where MedXit was stuck. The landing-page fight wasn't about a headline. It was the bill they were paying for a thousand small, unpriced decisions coming due. They needed what the pre-chosen black mock turtleneck gives: defaults that conserve brainpower for the non-default.

They needed a Belief OS.

We reconvened for a half-day session—not to debate beliefs, but to codify rules of engagement. Less refinery, more user manual. The session started with me asking them to answer some strategy questions. I was challenging them with hypothetical trade-offs—more budget on the GUI and user experience or easier middleware integration? Targeting hospitals geographically close, or focusing on less competitive regions? We brainstormed 25 potential principles that would codify and turn their Belief into actionable steps. We were looking for the practical answers to the multiple metaphorical versions of "What should I wear to work today?" Of the 20 or 30 potential decision-making principles we whittled it to a non-negotiable set of six.

How does this team navigate the obstacles in the Belief Gap while using the least amount of energy and deciding as quickly as possible? The answer to that question is to lock-in agreed upon decision making principles.

Here's what emerged:

Principle	Core Rule	Result
One Debate, One Decision	No "meeting after the meeting" or Slack back-channels.	Starves passive-aggression.
Data Over Opinions	Shift from "who's right" to "what data makes us right."	Conflict becomes co-investigation.
Disagree and Commit	Dissent is healthy during debate; undermining afterward is poison.	One face to the world.
Document the "Why"	Rationales live in a shared doc.	Preserves institutional memory.
Celebrate Good-Will Mistakes	Weekly "Golden Poop" awards for mistakes made in pursuit of the mission. (You'll see in Chapter 11)	Makes innovation survivable.
Time-Boxed Debates	Decide the duration of the argument upfront.	Drives momentum and action.

MedXit's metabolism changed just by installing those six criteria (they all agreed on) for each decision they make. Decision-Making Principles are speed. They're your black mock turtleneck. They also fit perfectly into the 30 minute BOODA stand-up meeting you'll read about in Chapter 10. But one gear was still missing, because like a puppy that wants to make every Air Jordan and Ferragamo his chew toy, Beliefs and Hypothesis need someone to keep a close eye on them.

This is applicable to even the most successful companies if they want to scale in hyper-growth.

Jeff Bezos discovered it the hard way. Even "two-pizza" teams get slow when leaders own ten projects at once.[2] So Amazon invented an internal laser sight: put one person in charge of one big bet and strip away everything else. They called that person the Single-Threaded Owner (STO). Bland title; radical practice.

An STO's world shrinks to a single outcome. No "also responsible for," no portfolio fog. Their job is binary: this thing lives or dies, and they're on the hook. They are the architects of the bridge that will get hundreds of others across the Belief Gap. That clarity accelerates the BOODA loop because there's no committee to gum up the works.

From my vantage point at ServerVault, I could see the contrast. We were proud engineers—pioneers in secure cloud—moving with deliberate care through a fragile ecosystem. Our creed: *Secure the Internet*. We engineered for "five nines" (99.999% uptime) when no one else was even close. Yet it was also while the market wanted "simple and ready before lunch." At the same time we were steadily growing, Andy Jassy at Amazon took their idle computing capacity and—single-threaded it into a unicorn. He turned all that hardware into the current market leader in cloud services, Amazon Web Services (AWS). Jassy didn't just have a good idea; he had the metabolism of an STO, which allowed AWS to outpace our "perfect caution" at ServerVault. We focused on refining and securing our service while they shipped and shipped. We didn't realize it at the time but we slowed our BOODA cycles, right as AWS compressed and accelerated theirs. It's humbling to admit, but in hindsight our perfect caution became a liability to hyper-growth and we were not going through the BOODA cycles quickly enough to see it. AWS became a juggernaut which we helped model and then couldn't catch, despite our four-year head-start.

Same story with Kindle. Dave Limp ran it like a garage startup inside a behemoth—tight team, direct reporting, rapid iteration. Not a side project; but a single obsession. STO isn't a title; it's a metabolism. He had to convince people both internally and externally a small screen the size of a birthday card could be produced so

---

2   The "two-pizza rule" is an organizational principle, famously used by Amazon, demanding that teams should be small enough to be fed by two large pizzas (roughly 6-10 people). This size constraint is intended to minimize communication overhead and bureaucracy, helping teams stay agile, autonomous, and accountable for their results.

that it was comfortable to read and could store hundreds of books. The delivery of a device and the popularity of the ecosystem were how he crossed the Belief Gap.

MedXit needed that same metabolism. After the landing-page fight, their new principles could carry them to a decision. But to move fast, they had to anoint Gio as STO of "Beta Tester Acquisition." Sandra and Shannon would weigh in during the one debate; then Gio would own the outcome. His rope to pull. His signature on the line.

III.

The screaming engines rattled my teeth. This was NASCAR pit lane, cars screeching down from 100 mph to 50 mph to 0 while halting on a precise stop-spot. Then before you can read this sentence, twenty people will have changed four tires. I was behind the wall at the Daytona 500 witnessing this speed firsthand. My company, ODIN, had branched out into a fan-engagement platform using RFID that we rolled out for NASCAR. I had all-access pass to the track (which was impressive) but it was pit lane that melted my brain. I immediately recognized the BOODA loop at ludicrous speed. It was adrenaline and awe.

Picture the alternative. The front-left tire tech decides to switch tire style mid-stop. The jack man argues with the gunner about new hand signals. The crew chief chats with the crew. The driver steps out for a coffee like *Talladega Nights*. Your two seconds turn into two minutes; your race turns into a comedy.

Pit crews can move as fast as they do because every decision is pre-made. Roles are crisp. Motions are choreographed. Contingencies are rehearsed. The job in the moment is not to decide; it's to act. One person, one job. Shared belief in process. Brutal efficiency in practice.

That's the promise of the Founder's Creed. The Shared Belief Map is your race strategy; the Decision-Making Principles are the rulebook; the STO is the crew chief over each make-or-break job. **Three simple tools that together, erase debate when speed is paramount, eliminate doubt when Belief is needed most.** This structure preserves time for healthy debate where it matters. The BOODA Doctrine turns a startup from a collection of opinions into a synchronized machine. Three simple tools in that Doctrine that will help you build a bridge across the Gap. This is the structure that will create Unicorns. I hope you are one of them.

There's also an industrial side of Belief you need to keep in mind as you scale for hyper-growth in your startup. You need to scale belief beyond your own four walls: you want to build a factory of Belief.

The best place to learn how to construct this factory is look at the Stata building—it's as if a couple of giants were playing a game of Jenga in Kendall Square, Cambridge. Just when the last piece gave way, the tumbling blocks froze in a playful spray of odd angles and bizarrely tilted walls. This building goes beyond beautiful architecture. It's more than one of the most recognizable buildings in the world. It shouts to the next incoming class of students—Believe in the impossible. Believe in yourself. Believe in MIT.

Figure 9—MIT's famous Stata Center is a beacon for creative audacity and possibility.

Inside MIT's campus of buildings is the famous Infinite Corridor, an 800-foot-long indoor path, protected from the elements of wintery Cambridge. On the walls along with upcoming events or announcements are stories and scars of past "hacks." What the public often calls pranks. A police car reassembled 50 feet up atop the Great Dome. Weather balloons blooming from under the turf at a Harvard-Yale football game with the MIT logo proudly emblazed. Elevators that only stopped at prime numbered floors during finals week. **Outsiders see**

pranks. Insiders see proofs: the world is malleable if you plan well and believe together.

Student founders have a unique advantage at top schools like MIT; they have established networks and extensive resources. At MIT, your roommate is your first beta tester, your professor your first advisor, and your alumni network your first cap table. Founder, and now VC, Pete Flint said student founders have a big benefit because *"When you're a student, the social graph is so tight that every win echoes through the network."* Hacks become belief-amplifiers because everyone's three feet away at the next desk.

It's not just hacks, there's also the famous MIT startup $100K competition. Ten minutes on stage to turn strangers into believers. The prize matters less than the nods and the applause. "Ridiculous" turns into "maybe" and "maybe" becomes oxygen. At universities around the world students are awash in resources—from super-computing time to soldering irons and CNC machines. Labs, mentors, alumni, even free pizza at hackathons add to the bounty. If a student needs something he or she can usually get it for free, often if they get something for free smart founders get paid to take it away. This uber-supportive environment makes it easier to start on an audacious idea and harder to stop. Living in a university eco-system gives student founders a big advantage. It reduces uncertainty at a time when you don't have to worry about paying rent or getting fired from your day job. It takes away worries of doubting colleagues and skeptical friends. Doubt doesn't kill you at MIT; it trains you to keep pushing.

A fixture at MIT is one of my favorite neuroscientists; Earl Miller who runs, the not-so-creatively-named Miller Lab at MIT. Earl is one of the most cited neuroscientists in the world, and a great bass player in a local band. Inside his lab, whiteboards have sketches of brain wave frequencies, experimental data, special dates. One of the areas Miller is famous for is his work on multi-tasking—a phenomenon which he has proven does not exist. He proved we switch tasks, focusing only on one at a time. According to Miller switching carries a tax. It slows you down because when you change from one thought to the other you have to "rewind" your thoughts a little bit to reestablish where you were. He also has a theory about spotlights and floodlights in your mind, you'll hear about later. But because of his research, MIT teaches students to focus like a brain surgeon on one task at a time. This is the kind of DNA that multiplies at places like MIT but isn't in the DNA of most startups, especially in this doom scrolling era that only is getting worse with AI. The question we need to ask is; how do our three founders at MedXit build that same passion, focus and grit as they cross their Belief Gap?

The first place to look is at the startups presenting at the $100k MIT competition. The winners know how they need to believe then they observe, orient and decide—by staying focused and not getting taxed by distractions. That's why MedXit leverages the SBM and Decision-Making Principles. Then, like the MIT students, they Act confidently. If you are working on two or three big projects at a time trying to cross the Gap, the best thing you can do is focus on one. Deliver, because the moment a prototype exists, belief stops being abstract; it becomes a thing the world can push back on and test. Dr. Karl Friston (my other favorite neuroscientist) from University College London created a theory called the Free Energy Principle (this is the why). You'll read more about him in Chapter 7, but he would say since **the brain is constantly trying to predict what happens next, when you're acting into the unknown you are buying prediction error on purpose.** You are getting comfortable with uncertainty. You're training your team. You are pushing past the unknown. Founders call it "shipping."

MIT is one giant greenhouse for belief. It engineers a hyper-growth climate: normalize audacity, ritualize public risk, institutionalize recovery. It helps people believe, like a greenhouse helps tomatoes get big and juicy even in the winter. A factory of belief produces not just culture but cadence.

If MIT is a greenhouse, Silicon Valley is the unbuffered wilderness. It's where a legend in Belief, and good friend of mine, Sami Inkinen, came to see what dent he could leave on the world. Sami and I met doing a mountain bike race about 15 years ago in Leadville, Colorado. Since then, we've done adventures on four continents together, probably because we're the only ones who believed that many of them were possible. Along with his wife, Meredith, and our friend Ray we won the Race Across America, cycling from California to Maryland as a four-person team. Many people didn't believe we could do the things we set out to do—but Sami always did. He has the quiet Finnish stubbornness of a man who knows how long miles feel and can always come up with some humor to ease the pain of those miles. Sami co-founded a company called Trulia in 2005 when "search for a home online" sounded like buying sushi through the mail. Real estate agents guarded their listings like the Coca-Cola recipe. At the time consumers trusted handshakes and glossy flyers, not pixels and browsers. The Belief Gap was a canyon.

Sami and his co-founder Pete Flint, who I mentioned earlier, built a bridge across that canyon one plank at a time. Scrape the data no one wanted to share. Clean it and organize it until transparency felt like magic. Put it in front of actual buyers and watch their faces when they realized they could browse neighborhoods without asking anyone's permission, without a nagging broker in the car with them, without even driving around. Every skeptical VC inspired their demo. Every hostile broker forced them to build a better wedge. This was BOODA in the wild: your critics pay you in data if you let them and if you are Observing closely enough to see value in their critiques.

Soon Sami and Pete were adding planks to their bridge: ten believers, fifty, a hundred, then five hundred. Journalists wrote. Analysts modeled. Venture Capitalists funded. Competitors rushed to copy ideas they'd made fun of just six months earlier. That's what crossing the Belief Gap feels like from the inside: slow and grinding, (Sami refers to it as eating glass every morning for breakfast) then suddenly, it becomes *inevitable*. Trulia's $3.5B merger with Zillow is the money headline; the real headline is cultural: a market dragged across by founders who refused to slow down their BOODA loop—speed was their imperative. They built, measured and nurtured culture through the kind of structures you're learning right now.

A quick cautionary detour. The Belief Glut is a comfortable island. Friendster built luxury condos on that island. They had first-mover advantage, lavish attention—then they stalled. Performance died, debates multiplied, decisions weren't made and users quietly left. Facebook crossed their gap by shipping, absorbing outrage when they introduced new features like the newsfeed, walking back just enough to keep most of the changes and then repeating that loop. The world says it wants stability; it rewards momentum. Netflix crossed the gap twice—DVDs by mail, then streaming—and made Blockbuster aisles feel like wax museums, or more accurately a hallway in one of those Friendster condos.

Belief unshared is hallucination. Belief multiplied is traction.

You don't need MIT's Infinite Corridor to build a factory of Belief. You need to leverage your own BOODA doctrine and rhythm:

1. **Write the creed (one page).** Always / Never / Trade-offs. If your team can't recite it, it doesn't exist.
2. **Draw the Shared Belief Map.** Separate Core Beliefs (load-bearing beams) from Hypotheses (the ornate trim around the windows). Update monthly. Publish. Share.

3. **Recruit the first ten.** You're not winning a debate; you're inviting courage. You're squashing doubt. Make bravery cheap with tiny proofs that add up. Remember external acolytes are more valuable than internal—especially if they are paying for what you make.

4. **Install short loops.** Daily Decide → Act. Weekly: one outcome that moved. Monthly: one hypothesis upgraded (or downgraded) and replaced.

5. **Normalize recovery.** Postmortems that praise clarity. "Golden Poop" Award for the expensive insight when someone makes a mistake that generates data. (You'll learn more in Chapter 11)

6. **Build public proof.** Hacks, demos, pilots, fake-door tests, or clinical trials. People believe what they can point at, what they can touch and feel.

7. **Measure believers.** Count humans who crossed the Gap: activations, renewals, partners who staked reputation, analysts who took a demo, journalists who gave you a couple lines in an article. Revenue lags belief so find other things to measure. Sami and Pete at Trulia measured the culture with quarterly surveys asking the team how they were doing on their six principles of culture. They could see their performance.

8. **Guard against the Glut.** Monthly Gap Audit: *Who outside this room joined us this month?* Few names should sound the alarm. A few months of no additions means Orient to what you are seeing in a new way - time to pivot or shut down, if you really want hyper-growth.

9. **Appoint stewards.** Belief that depends on you dies with your calendar. Steward the creed; don't cosplay the founder.

10. **Name STOs.** Two or three rocks you're focused on. One name per rock. Portfolios are where urgency goes to nap, so keep it lean and accountable.

That sunny afternoon in Cambridge, we walked back into MedXit with their new doctrine in hand. And we used it right away. Here's how it worked on the new site marketing action:

Step 1 - One debate, one decision: we time-boxed the landing-page argument for 45 minutes, we set the clock. The purpose was to decide just on the landing page options, nothing more.

Step 2 - Data over opinions: we created an A/B-test of two landing page versions—Sandra's clinical promise vs. Gio's bold hook reframed to *"Feel markedly better in 30 days—measured."*

Step 3 - Disagree and commit: Debate and then one person decides. In this case, the call was Gio's as the STO. Everyone made their arguments and tried to persuade each other for the 45 minutes we time-boxed it. Then at 43 minutes, Gio had to decide since he was the owner. After his decision, the whole leadership team signed the commitment in the doc. Agree or not, they were all committed to support the choice, end of discussion.

Step 4 - Document the why: Take the time now, to put in some structure and reap the benefits later. The why - rationale, risk, metrics in one page.

Step 5 - Celebrate good-will mistakes: We would see in the next week or two if Gio whiffed, if so, and he struck out, the Golden Poop (You'll meet in Chapter 11) is his to win with a smile. It took a lot of pressure off, and at the same time no one really wants a painted piece of shit as an award, so Gio was putting in his best effort.

Reminder: Time-box: forty five minutes to decide, then forty-eight hours to ship. In this case they would start the A/B testing within 48 hours through a series of Meta and Google ads. This was a unified team, all moving aggressively in one direction and if they keep their BOODA cycles they will have new data in 48 hours and can start running through another cycle.

It felt like a NASCAR pit stop. Two seconds of metaphorical tire changing stretched to two days to deliver an A/B test, and the energy was the same: no new decisions in the lane, no confusion or debate. The pre-work did its job. The car rolled out. The world answered. We updated the creed. MedXit crushed it, they got through the BOODA loop even faster than we thought. The next day the A/B ads were up on google—they compressed the loop from 48 hours to 24 and in 36 hours we had statistically significant data. That's operational hygiene—nothing getting in the way, nothing messing up the cogs.

Speed, in the end, isn't frantic. It's frictionless.

A very effective agenda for a BOODA Stand-Up is simple, effective and fast.

Objective: Replace organizational chaos with a disciplined cadence of execution.

Step	Section	Time	Key Focus	Output / Action
1	The Creed Check-In	2 Min	Alignment: Anchoring the team to the mission, repeat it out loud.	Review the Shared Belief Map (SBM) to ensure everyone is seeing the same reality.
2	STO Outcome Reports	10 Min	Velocity: Single-Threaded Owners (STOs) report using "Verbs Only."	Report on what was Done, Observed, and Learned since the last loop.
3	The Dissonance Filter	10 Min	Decisiveness: Identifying "Herbie" (the bottlenecks) and forcing movement.	Execute the 70% Rule: Decide with available data to reduce uncertainty.
4	The Golden Poop	3 Min	Culture: Turning expensive mistakes into institutional doctrine.	Publicly award the person whose well-intentioned error generated the best data.
5	Action Comm-itment	5 Min	Momentum: Setting a discrete move to beat the next trip around the sun.	Every owner commits to one specific action to be completed within 24 or 48 hours.

The BOODA Doctrine isn't a TED Talk about belief. It's a way to manufacture belief at scale, it is the most important ingredient to a successful, hyper-growth company. This holds true even if, like at Amazon, you are starting something entirely new at a behemoth company. I remember my first job after grad school with the largest real estate provider in the country, Trammell Crow. I was tasked with starting a technology practice on the East Coast to focus on data centers. Many people internally thought it was a waste of time, the Internet wouldn't go beyond a few big businesses. I had a big Belief Gap to get people across *internally* as well as externally. Intrapreneurship has founders too; they just happen to be part of a 1,000 person company. Your Shared Belief Map is the what. Your decision principles are the rulebook, the how. Your STOs are the crew chiefs, the who. Your rituals compress the loop until your company stops being a plan and becomes a verb. That's when you can *Uber* home and get some rest.

As you're speeding home in your Uber, keep in mind the goal isn't just to build a fast car. It's to build a team that can service that car in two seconds, in the rain, with cameras on, while competitors analyze why you're already a lap ahead. The Belief Gap is the racetrack; your principles and ownership are what let you fly through the turns. You move so quickly your rivals assume they missed something obvious and schedule another meeting to find and debate it.

Let them. You'll be back on the track, looping BOODA like Richard Petty at the Daytona 500—again and again, until what started as your private conviction becomes everyone else's new normal.

What I've learned watching hundreds of founders try to cross their own Belief Gaps, is that speed and cadence and methodology don't create culture. They might create habits or methods, but they don't build culture. Belief does. And when belief is shared, it creates something far rarer than speed: it builds belonging.

Most people join startups for the adventure. They want to feel the rush of the unknown, to be part of something that matters, to help will a vision into existence, sure there might be a golden ticket at a sale or IPO, but Investment Banking or Consulting is a much safer way to earn a lot of money so there must be something else. What makes your early believers stay isn't equity or kombucha on tap—it's that moment when they look around and realize, *I'm with my people.*

The BOODA Doctrine doesn't just build alignment; it builds that feeling. It's a belonging engine disguised as an operating system. When your team maps out its Shared Beliefs together, you're not just agreeing on strategy—you're drawing your family crest. Every time you argue through Decision Principles, you're teaching each other how to disagree without breaking trust. Every Golden Poop moment—someone screwing up in pursuit of the mission and getting applauded for it—tells the whole room, *You can fail here and still belong.*

There's neuroscience behind that warmth, that belonging, that safety. Earl Miller at MIT calls it *shared predictive coding*: when a group sees the same reality, their brains literally sync up. It's the biological basis of trust. The BOODA Loop—Believe, Observe, Orient, Decide, Act—is more than a process; it's a rhythm. **When a team runs it together, doubt gets metabolized into motion. That rhythm is belonging.**

I saw this at ODIN years ago. It was 2009 and we were in the middle of a death march toward a launch—too little sleep, too many bugs, and way too much caffeine. Our main conference of the year, The RFID Journal Live event in Orlando, was coming up and we were launching a revolutionary new system we designed for the US Special Operations Command. It was an engineering marvel that even included our own chips, and proprietary antennas, all in a form factor no one had ever dreamed of before. But the whole team was fried. One night, around 2 a.m., a junior engineer pushed a bad bit of code onto the reader module that crashed the system. You could almost hear the oxygen get sucked out of our big warehouse lab. Then our head of engineering, Chetan, instead of yelling, slapped the guy on the back and said, "Great! Now we know that doesn't work. Deploy the fix and document it." Ten minutes later, the whole team was laughing, pizza boxes open, music back up to full volume and the lab was humming along. That was belonging. Not because everything went right—but because it didn't, and no one bailed, no one judged. We ended the night (or morning really) putting dry ice in a water tank, inside a shipping container with me locked in at the same time, so we could practice dramatically opening the door for my Bono moment at the conference when we released the technology. I planned on strutting out of the container in a swirl of rising fog carrying our SMART Container system. It was bad ass—and the live launch ended up being off the charts. We won the Best-In-Show award that year. The pride was shared among every person in the company. And pride in what you do lasts a lot longer than money or stock.

Founders spend so much energy chasing talent (sometimes great talent, sometimes "right now" talent) that they forget what deep, mature humans really want. It's not perks. It's purpose. People don't want to work *for* your company; they want to work *inside* your creed. They want to know that their mistakes, their ideas, and their courage all count toward something and that something is being part of a team crossing the Belief Gap together. It's about facing those obstacles and giving the person next to you a leg up before you pull yourself over. The BOODA Doctrine gives them purpose. It's not just how you scale belief; it's how you build a home you can be proud of. But as the MedXit team was about to find out, a home filled with believers is only the beginning. When Belief turns into a huge grant and a rewrite of the national healthcare playbook, the question changes. You've built the race car; now, can you keep the tires from spinning off?

4

Living the Creed

I.

I got a call from Gio at MedXit—he was breathless. "Great news! We just won a $700,000 grant, and the largest hospital in Massachusetts is rewriting an RFP so that it fits our specific technology. The Shared Belief Map (SBM) and our Decision-Making Principles are really working."

Then came the anxiety I see in almost every successful founder. "But now we have to deliver. This is the hyper-growth we wanted, but I need to track three or four projects now. It's pulling me away from being a true Single-Threaded Owner (STO). How can we build the team for the future, not just for right now?"

It was the perfect question for a founder to ask. If they wanted to double in size in the next twelve months, they couldn't just work harder; they had to shift from leading with control to leading with context.

I told him about a win at ODIN that taught me more about the power of a shared creed than any time I could have spent at IBM or McKinsey. We had gone after the first major RFID contract Airbus ever issued—a massive RFP to track the entire supply chain and work-in-process for the A380. We were a small, tough team from Virginia going up against IBM, Motorola, and a field of multi-billion-dollar incumbents.

On paper, we were way outgunned. But we didn't sell Airbus diagrams or buzz-words; we sold them conviction. At ODIN, one of our Core Beliefs was that 99.9% read accuracy wasn't aspirational; it was table stakes. We had done it repeatedly, and our RFP response reflected that conviction. That unmistakable confidence didn't just help us win—it annihilated competitors with far more resources.

When I met Carlo, the young executive leading the RFID initiative at Airbus headquarters in Toulouse, I realized he was an intrapreneur trying to cross his own Belief Gap inside a massive, risk-averse organization. He needed a partner who operated with the speed of belief, not the drag of bureaucracy. The same was true for MedXit.

"Gio," I said, "the danger as you scale isn't the number of projects. It's that as complexity grows, Belief often gets replaced by 'corporate paste'—the layers of process that stifle high-performers. To show him what was at stake, I sketched out the reality of organizational gravity on a napkin at the cafe where we met.

"In the mid-1990s, Reed Hastings was living your nightmare at a company called Pure Atria. It was successful and heading for an IPO, but Hastings was miserable. He was managing a 'normal company' where people followed processes, filled out expense reports, and generally did what they were told. Creativity was stifled by bureaucracy because high-performers were being dragged down by their 'good-enough' co-workers. They were playing not-to-lose. Hastings wanted to play to win, and that required a radical new approach to their Creed."

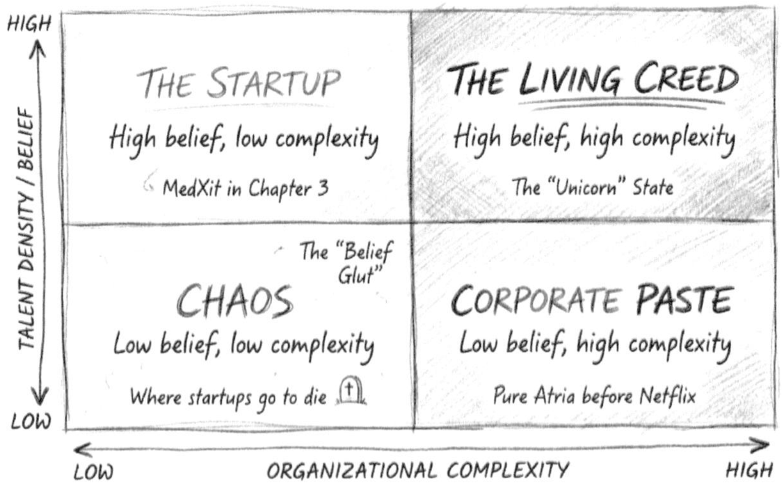

Figure 10—Belief or Bureaucracy are the two roads a promising startup can follow.

Hastings realized that to move into that top-right quadrant, he didn't need a bigger HR department; he needed more powerful purpose and principles. He says that his epiphany came during a merger. His company acquired a smaller company, and Hastings had to integrate the two engineering teams. His team was methodical, process-driven, and predictable. The other team was like a chaotic band of brilliant, cocky, argumentative, and incredibly talented fighter pilots. Hastings, a man who valued order and process above all else, found himself secretly admiring the fighter pilots. They were more innovative, more passionate, and frankly, more effective. Reflecting on the differences in company culture, he wondered how Pure Atria lost its spark. The moment also planted a seed in his mind: what if you could build a company that was only Jet Jockeys like Maverick and Ice Man? What if you could build a team composed entirely of super high-octane colleagues, and what if you could give them the freedom to operate without the soul-crushing rules of a "normal" company? Initially most founders worry about the fact that it would be the ultimate chaos spinning quickly out of control—Iceman and Maverick at each other's throats all the time arguing about the silliest details. But Hastings proved them wrong. It took a 125-slide presentation to do it.

This question of hiring only Top Gun pilots became the foundational creed for his next venture: a DVD-by-mail service called Netflix. From its inception, Netflix was designed as an explicit rejection of the corporate norms Hastings had come to despise. He and his co-founder, Marc Randolph, were not just building a business; they were filling a life size Pietri dish with an experiment of organizational design. Their goal was to create a high-performance culture that could sustain hyper-growth and innovation for years on end without being crippled by the twin diseases of complexity and mediocrity.

The result of this experiment was one of the most famous and controversial documents in business history: the Netflix Culture Deck. This document, originally intended for internal use only, laid out, in brutally honest detail, the company's core philosophy. It wasn't a collection of feel-good platitudes about teamwork and integrity. It was a stark, unsentimental operating manual for a professional sports team. It famously declared, "We are a team, not a family." It outlined its core values not as aspirations, but as concrete, observable behaviors, such as "You say what you think, even if it is controversial," and "You are candid about performance." It made it clear that merely "adequate" performance would be met with a generous severance package. The document was what moved them from control to context—Hastings didn't have a big HR department and forms to fill out for days off, he had a statement "No vacation policy—you are an adult you should know when to work and when to rest." He gave the team context "you are an adult" instead of "you need HR approval and must fill out these forms."

When the deck was leaked, it went viral. Sheryl Sandberg (was then a high-level executive at Google and would go on to become the COO of Facebook) called it "the most important document ever to come out of Silicon Valley." It was downloaded millions of times. It was debated, copied, and many people seem horrified by its Machiavellian tone. To others, it was a refreshingly honest blueprint for building a high performing organization. To others, it was a recipe for a cutthroat, psychologically unsafe dystopia.

But whether you loved it or hated it, you couldn't deny its power. The Netflix Culture Deck was more than just a presentation. It was an act of indoctrination. It was a tool designed with a single, ruthless purpose: to attract the right people, repel the wrong ones, and ensure that every single person who walked through the doors of Netflix understood and subscribed to its unique and demanding creed, the creed that was rocketing them across the Belief Gap. Hastings wasn't just looking for employees; he was recruiting Believers.

The Culture Deck was Netflix's Shared Belief Map, supercharged for talent acquisition. It was a record of their internal reality, a clear signal sent out to the world that said, "This is who we are. This is how we operate. If this resonates with you, we want you. If it doesn't, for the love of God, please go work somewhere else." They were looking for fighter pilots who felt comfortable around other, shit-talking, speed-loving, G-force pulling fighter jocks. In the deck they show the difference between reality and the normal corporate blah, blah, blah that doesn't mean anything in practice. It's not enough to have a creed if it's never implemented.

There are countless stories of useless corporate speak blabbering in the halls of many failed companies who didn't follow a creed. Having a creed or values doesn't mean anything if they aren't lived every moment of every day. One of the biggest corporate failures of all time proved just that. In the lobby of their headquarters proudly hung the corporate values. "Integrity, Communication, Respect and Excellence." Everyone who walked in the door walked past their "values." Those four words, however, were most definitely not what was valued at Enron. The once high-flying darling of Wall Street avalanched into the largest bankruptcy in US history. They were perpetrating accounting fraud to keep weak financial results looking strong. More than 30 employees were convicted of felonies related to the fraud. How is that for Integrity? Words on a wall don't create culture or a creed.

The Netflix deck points out that "The actual company values (as opposed to the nice-sounding values) are shown by who gets rewarded, promoted, or let go. Actual company values are the behaviors and skill that are valued in fellow employees." Then the document goes on to explain the nine behaviors and skills that are critical to be part of the team. MedXit had to figure out how to create body-part rejection for a new hire that didn't fit, and that didn't whole-heartedly believe in the MedXit creed. They didn't want anyone in the organization contributing to corporate paste as they grew.

Many founders underestimate the challenge of keeping the culture alive during hyper-growth. That's why so many companies look promising after their Seed and Series A round and then just fade into oblivion, even with a disruptive or innovative product that people are buying. They have money to hire but not the structure to hire and on-board optimally. It's a challenge that every founder faces once they have forged their own creed and received some market validation. Without the real-life values being understood and enforced and rewarded then, like at Enron, they are nothing more than letters on the wall.

Figure 11—You must have that strong unambiguous mission as the foundation

A significant problem with raising money at this tenuous stage of the company development is you get professional investors as board members, and often they don't know a damn thing about the challenges going from a 10 person company to 25 people then from 25 to 100 seemingly overnight. The inexperienced investor phenomenon is especially true in Europe where less than 15% of Venture Capitalists were company founders. In the USA more than half of the VC funds have historically had founders on their teams.

Another value of the SBM and defining the decision-making framework is that problems can be directly addressed even across different geographies. One thing I found while working for an Italian venture capital firm is that very few employees have seen wildly successful startups first-hand. The smartest graduates from top European Schools like Bocconi or Polytechnique in Milan or EPFL in Switzerland historically take the highest paying, most stable position they can get from the biggest, best known companies. That's an old-school home run for them. Mamma and Pappa are so proud, bravo!

If two guys in a garage offer the same top graduates a miserable salary but a bunch of equity, because these European graduates have little or no frame of reference, they turn down the opportunity. If those two guys making the offer are the next Steve Jobs and Steve Wasniak then our top graduate made a billion dollar mistake by not becoming employee number three. This is another area where the Belief Gap concept is so critical to teach your team and the people crossing with you, especially the non-US based employees. You have to get them uncharacteristically passionate about your Belief, too.

How do you make sure that the sometimes fragile, hard-won alignment of the Founding Team isn't instantly diluted as you get bigger? How do you scale Belief?

This is the work of indoctrination. This is what the US Military does during basic training and then later at flight school—it's the pre-cursor to the OODA loop that makes the BOODA Doctrine so powerful for those outside the military. But let's be clear: we are not talking about brainwashing. We are talking about the deliberate, systematic process of embedding your company's Core Beliefs and operating principles into every step of the employee lifecycle, from the first job description they read to the last exit interview they give.

You must be ready for a focused effort to turn your culture from a byproduct of who you happen to hire into your single most powerful and defensible competitive advantage—the Belief.

You don't just build a product; you build a hyper-scalable machine that builds a product, provides a service, or saves the world. Of course, that machine is your people, because thanks to the SBM everyone is aligned, all executing on the same creed. The Founder's Creed.

II.

Let's go back to our team at MedXit. They have their Shared Belief Map pinned to the wall. They have their set of Decision-Making Principles on everyone's laptop. The engine is humming. Now, they need to hire their first non-founding employee: a Head of Marketing.

Before discovering the BOODA Doctrine, their process would have looked familiar to anyone who has ever hired for a startup. They would have written a generic job description filled with corporate buzzwords ("fast-paced environment," "dynamic team," "self-starter wanted."). They would have screened resumes for impressive logos and fancy degrees. They would have conducted a series of unstructured interviews, asking predictable questions like "What's your biggest weakness?" and ultimately decided who to hire based on a vague, subjective feeling of "culture fit." Even if you give them a homework assignment, which I did with hundreds of people I hired, you still would have been hiring for skill and experience, hoping that belief would somehow magically follow, or maybe rub off on them due to proximity of the founders. Would you get the Fighter Pilot or the grunt carrying around chocks looking for a wheel to stuff them under?

That old school approach to hiring is like putting a regulator on hyper-growth. You are applying the brakes, whether you mean to or not. It's like that pit crew looking for a new jack operator. They see the resume that he was on Formula 1 pit crew for five years, and hope that those skills translate to NASCAR. You don't just add a person to the team; you are adding their entire belief system, their ingrained habits, and their personal operating system to your delicate ecosystem. Do you want Ricky Bobby or Jean Girard's Beliefs? Both are great drivers, but they have very different views of the world. If your choice is not a match with your creed, the friction will be immediate and corrosive. The challenge is it's often not corrosive enough to let someone go right away, even though you should.

With the Founder's Creed as their guide, MedXit takes a radically different approach. Their goal is not just to hire a Head of Marketing; it is to find the *perfect* Head of Marketing for *their* specific creed. The process is no longer about assessing skills; it is about assessing alignment. It is an act of indoctrination that begins long before the first interview.

Step 1: Weaponize the Job Description

The first point of contact a candidate has with your company is the job description. Most companies treat this as a bureaucratic chore. A company living its creed treats it as its primary recruiting weapon. You want people to say "No way" as quickly as possible. Because if you lay everything out on the first point of engagement and set expectations, you'll save yourself a lot of time and money. Eventually you will get someone who says, "Hell yeah!" and then you know you've got the right candidate. Resilience is a big key here for your hiring manager, or what Angela Duckworth coined *Grit*[1]—not blind perseverance, but the willingness to stay in the fight when their ideas are challenged, their ego takes a hit, and the work gets uncomfortable, so you need someone tough.

MedXit's new job description for their Head of Marketing looks nothing like its generic predecessor. It is a miniature manifesto, it's like an elevator pitch equivalent of Netflix's Culture Deck. The first paragraph doesn't list requirements; it states the company's mission and Core Beliefs, front and center, taken directly from their SBM. It explicitly describes their culture of debate, critique and their "Data Over Opinions" principle. It includes a sentence like, "If you are uncomfortable with having your best ideas rigorously challenged in a search for the truth, this is not the right role for you."

The job description acts as the first important filter. It is designed to make the right candidate's heart beat faster and to make the wrong candidate roll their eyes and close the browser tab. It saves everyone time. It begins the cultural training process by forcing candidates to self-select based on their alignment with the creed, not just their qualifications. Reed Hastings did this brilliantly. The Netflix Culture Deck acted as a 125 slide, public job description that pre-qualified millions of potential candidates without a single recruiter having to lift the phone or bang out an email.

Step 2: The Creed Interview

The interview process is no longer a series of polite, meandering conversations. It

---

[1]   Duckworth, Angela. Grit: The Power of Passion and Perseverance. New York: Scribner, 2016

is a structured, systematic stress-test designed to probe a candidate's alignment with the company's Decision-Making Principles. The evaluation focuses on Data, Commitment and Ownership. Every founder at MedXit is involved, and each is assigned a specific principle to test.

Sandra, the doctor, is tasked with assessing the candidate's commitment to "Data Over Opinions." Instead of asking, "Tell me about a successful campaign you ran," she asks, "Tell me about a time you had a strong conviction about a marketing strategy that the data proved wrong. What did you do?"

She is not listening for the outcome of the story; she is listening for the process. Or do they try to explain away the data and cling to their original anecdotal opinion? This old school attitude was what killed baseball scouts—if you haven't, read Money Ball by Michael Lewis he does a masterful job of highlighting the failure of opinion over data and those dinosaurs who clung to their opinions. Now let's go on to the second interview.

Giovanni, the business guy is the right one to test the "Disagree and Commit" belief, he wants to know if this candidate can put the team ahead of her ego. He presents her with a real-life scenario: the debate he and Sandra had over the "Add three years to your life" headline. He then asks, "Imagine you were in my shoes. You believe the bold headline is the right call, but the team decides to go with Sandra's more conservative option. What do you do next? He is looking for a very specific answer. A mediocre candidate will waffle or try to find a compromise. A great candidate will say something like, "First, I would argue passionately for my position in the meeting, I'm opinionated, like most successful executives and I will make my best argument. But once the decision is made, my job is to make the chosen headline the most successful headline in the history of marketing." That's a winner in interview number two. The third interview dives deeper into teamwork.

Shannon, the engineer, is tasked with assessing the candidate's view on teamwork and ownership, using a question designed to sniff out any tendency toward social loafing. She asks, "Tell me about the most successful project you've ever been a part of. What was your specific, individual contribution? What part of it could not have happened without you?" This question forces the candidate to move beyond the collective "we" and articulate their personal, tangible impact. It's a search for single-threaded owners, not passengers. She is looking for things the candidate caught that her team might have missed, a nuance that isn't part of the text-book methodology that had a big impact. She is looking for someone with the confidence and courage to want, in fact need, a meritocracy. So one of the other things Shannon will probe for is how did the candidate challenge someone more senior to them in an organization—their boss or even their boss's boss.

This entire process, which takes place over several interviews, builds a multi-dimensional picture of the candidate. MedXit is no longer guessing at "culture fit." They are gathering concrete data points on the candidate's alignment with their most deeply held beliefs and behaviors. If any one of the three founders becomes sure they are not going to hire this person, then they change perspective and start to sell the vision and potential of the company. They want the candidate leaving saying—those guys are incredible. They want rejected candidates saying great things to their friends as well. If each founder loves the candidate they sell the role and the opportunity.

The last step for MedXit was something we first incorporated at ODIN. It's a homework assignment. The person who is hiring a new team member was the one responsible for giving the candidates a homework assignment that was not to exceed eight hours of prep time. The homework was specific to real world challenges we faced, and particularly relevant to the team they wanted to join. In general, there are five components to a good homework assignment that also helps with the indoctrination and building up their Belief.

The five criteria are:

Open-Ended but Constrained
Set a clear objective but leave the path open to test creativity and prioritization, and make sure they are aware of the time limit.

Real-World Relevance
Mirror real tasks your team tackles — not puzzles or theory. Be sure the leader of the group tasked with hiring, puts a few traps in there that you'd only know if you worked at the company, or if you looked beyond the traditional methodology.

Structured Inputs, Unstructured Outputs
Provide just enough structure (context, goals, data) to see how they deal with ambiguity, when they ask how you want the results returned let them know it's up to them.

Optional Collaboration
Offer a chance to "phone a friend" or simulate collaboration, testing humility and

team spirit. This is one reason you put a trap or two in the problem so that they will have to seek collaboration to really nail the answer.

Self-Assessment Prompt
Ask them to finish by answering the question: "What would you do differently with more time or support?"

Hiring the right person is like finding a potent chemical element. It's valuable, but inert. The work isn't done. The real challenge is sparking the reaction that integrates them into the complex molecular structure of your company. This is onboarding, it's known in the military as indoctrination. And most startups get it disastrously wrong.

A normal company's onboarding process involves a tour of the office, a mountain of HR paperwork, and a series of awkward introductory meetings. It's a process of administrative assimilation. At ODIN, I learned that the first 90 days are the most critical period for indoctrination, at the end of three months you want every employee to have the highest level possible of Belief, they had to live our creed. This is the time when initial belief is either forged in iron or forsaken. Our approach wasn't about assimilation; it's about Belief *activation*.

Activation is built on a deeply counterintuitive principle that makes most founders uncomfortable, because it's the opposite of what you, a founder, should do: Micromanage the onboarding, delegate the role, empower the person.

The temptation after hiring a superstar Head of Marketing is to toss them the keys and say, "You're the expert, go figure it out." For a founder (especially one suffering from a touch of imposter syndrome, as all of us do at some point) delegation feels like the right, respectful thing to do. Several of the companies you've read about so far believe that letting the new hire just figure it out is, in fact, an act of abdication that sets that new hire up for failure, or at the very least sets them up to do less than their best. Take Trulia for example, Sami and Pete were not marketing gurus, they were physicists and new business school graduates. But when they hired a world-class marketing expert, they were confident the expert knew marketing but they, the founders, were the world-class experts on *Trulia*. Their primary job was to transfer their unique context and background with the speed and precision of a John Boyd military briefing. They had to fill up the Marketing expert's fuel tank for an endurance event, one that was full of sprints and that new hire needed to know the when and why behind the Trulia way.

So, the new Head of Marketing MedXit just hired doesn't get a laptop and a welcome packet on day one. They receive a 10-page, single-spaced document, personally written by Sandra and Giovanni. It's not an employee handbook. It's a mission dossier. It is the new hire's personalized roadmap for their first 60 days, designed to compress years of Founder's learning into weeks. It has four sections:

1. **Top Three Focus Areas:** The document starts by cutting through the noise. It doesn't list ten priorities; it lists the three or four mountains that absolutely must be climbed in the next six months that fall under the category of Marketing (some people like the term 'Rocks' from Steven Covey the author of "7 Habits of Highly Effective People.[2]") If possible you can narrow the Focus down to a Single Thread for the new hire– one primary focus. For MedXit Head of Marketing, it's: 1. Validate the "Beta Tester" hypothesis by acquiring 1,000 users (Gio is the STO for that one). 2. Build the initial data engine to prove the "Data Over Opinions" principle (Shannon own this). 3. Craft the core brand story to cross the Belief Gap with investors (The new Head of Marketing is the STO for this). There is no ambiguity about what victory looks like.

2. **Quarterly Initiatives & Time Allocations:** Giovanni breaks those mountains down into specific, high-leverage campaigns. For Q1, he allocates 40% of the new hire's budget and focus on a targeted social campaign for beta testers, and 20% on setting up analytics. This isn't a straitjacket; it's a strategic starting point based on the founders' hard-won knowledge of the landscape, there is history to short-cut the Marketing Head's ramp-up.

3. **The Meeting Sequence:** Shannon, the engineer who values efficiency, has choreographed the first four weeks of meetings for the new hire. It's not a random series of meet-and-greets. It's a sequenced transfer of knowledge. Week one is for meetings with the founders to internalize the Creed. Week two is for meetings with the product team to understand the technology. Week three is for listening to customer calls. She's not just building a calendar; she is architecting the new hire's

---

2   Covey would place a glass jar, a few big rocks, some pebbles, and sand before his class and ask if they could all fit. Most said no—when they added sand first, then pebbles, there was no room for the rocks. Then he'd reverse the order: rocks first, then pebbles, then sand filling the gaps. They all fit. The lesson? Focus on the big things first—the rocks.

internal network for maximum impact.

4. **Lessons Learned & Institutional Knowledge:** In a moment of radical transparency, Sandra has written a section titled, "Mines We've Already Stepped On." It's a brutally honest list of failed marketing experiments, dead-end messaging, and hard-won customer insights. It's the company's scar tissue, offered up as a gift. It saves the new hire from making the same mistakes and accelerates their learning curve exponentially.

This intensive process culminates in the most crucial and unorthodox step. On Day 60, the new Head of Marketing doesn't *receive* a performance review. They *give* one. Sandra, Shannon and Giovanni would all sit and listen as the new Marketing Head shared a fresh perspective on the company. More data.

The leadership team asked the new head of marketing to present on one topic: "The Company I See." They deliver a candid assessment of the team, the strategy, the culture, and the product. They point out the sacred cows, the dumb processes, and the unspoken truths everyone else is too close to see. This isn't just a feedback session; it's the final stage of the activation. It's the moment empowerment becomes real. The founders have given the new hire the full context of the company's past and present; now, the new hire is empowered to help design its future.

If you ignore new hires, or "delegate" too early, you're basically handing a wrench to a surgeon in the middle of an operations. Add a believer but don't indoctrinate them, and you've taken your first step toward killing hyper-growth momentum.

I get it, you are so focused on fund-raising, finishing the MVP, deploying the first pilot; you're swamped. For many founders putting a system in a place to scale on-boarding is on the yellow Post-It list under a wet coffee cup. Training new recruits doesn't seem to first time founders as the best use of their time—after all they are hiring an expert in just one particular discipline, that dude better know his job, because you've got so many other fires to put out, right? Wrong.

How you handle the first 60 days of a key new hire like the Head of Marketing, makes the difference between hiring an employee and forging a Believer. You haven't just added a jack operator to the pit crew. You've taken a skilled driver, run them through an intensive track simulator, shared the complete race plan, shown past crashes and wins, revealed the strengths and weakness of each competitor, and then, finally, handed them the steering wheel. Now they are ready to race. The only problem the MedXit team was facing was how do they know if their on-boarding and leveraging their Creed was working. Revenue and profit are easy, but they miss the critical foundational understanding of whether the Doctrine was working because they were not sure how to measure the unmeasurable. Lucky for them they have a north star in the healthcare industry. Before you meet her, however, you're going to hear more what happens when this incredible team you are putting together starts to feel the little gnawing of doubt as they steadily navigate their way through the Belief Gap.

5

The Alchemy of Doubt

I.

You met Sami Inkinen in the last chapter, the quiet Finn with a reservoir of stubbornness deep enough to row across oceans and build two unicorns from scratch. You saw how he and his co-founder at Trulia crossed the Belief Gap by patiently laying one plank of data at a time until a skeptical real estate industry had no choice but to walk across their bridge. That was a canyon. But for his next act, Sami chose to take on a challenge so vast, so fortified by institutional dogma, that it made the real estate problem at Trulia look like a crack in the sidewalk. He chose to take on the equivalent of the Grand Canyon as his Belief Gap.

This new venture, Virta Health, was founded on a belief so radical it sounded like medical heresy. The establishment had its decades-old creed, held with the certainty of religious law, that was simple: Type 2 diabetes is a chronic, progressive disease. You *manage* it. You write prescriptions for insulin, bill insurance companies, and refill those prescriptions for the rest of the patient's life. Entire industries—pharmaceutical giants, massive hospital systems, insurance empires, and the regulatory bodies that oversee them—were built on the back of that single, unquestioned belief. It wasn't just a business model; it was the consensus reality.

Virta's creed was a direct assault on that existing reality: Type 2 diabetes could be *reversed*.

When Sami walked into a room to pitch this idea, he wasn't just presenting a business plan; he was challenging a worldview. You could see the cognitive dissonance ripple across the faces of investors. Doctors, trained for decades in the management model, called the approach irresponsible. Regulators raised eyebrows at best and threatened subpoenas at worst.

For Virta, doubt wasn't an obstacle on the side of the road. It *was* the road. Every single step forward required confronting a universe screaming that the Virta way was impossible. This was the Belief Gap in its most formidable form—not a chasm between a founder and a few skeptical investors, but a canyon separating a new belief from the entire medical-industrial complex, a massive wall of doubt.

And yet, Virta is crossing it. They haven't done it by bulldozing the wall of doubt. They did it by absorbing it. They treated every obstacle not as a barrier, but as raw material to find their way. Every skeptical doctor's question became a data point that sharpened their clinical trial design. Every "that will never work" from an insurer became the impetus to gather more evidence and publish more peer-reviewed papers. Sami calls Virta a movement, because movements don't erase obstacles. They recruit them. The very doubt that was supposed to kill them became the force that made their arguments stronger, their data more robust, and their belief more unshakable. They understood a secret that separates the companies that change the world from those that just have good ideas. The paradox of the Belief Gap is this: the very walls that block you are also the pillars you can use to build your bridge.

II.

Two thousand years before Sami Inkinen battled insurance companies, the most powerful man in the world sat in a tent on the cold plains of Germania, leading a war against invading tribes, and scribbled a note to himself in his journal, in what became to be known as his meditations. He wasn't trying to secure FDA approval or close a Series B, but he was wrestling with the same fundamental challenge: how to move forward when the world pushes back.

His name was Marcus Aurelius, the Roman Emperor, and his private note has become one of the most powerful and enduring principles of strategy and resilience ever written:

"The impediment to action advances action. What stands in the way becomes the way."

This isn't a flowery aphorism. It's an operating system. Ryan Holiday's blockbuster book, *The Obstacle Is the Way*, built an entire philosophy for modern life on this single Stoic idea, because it contains a profound psychological reframe that is essential for any founder. It teaches you to see obstacles not as interruptions to your plan, but as integral parts of it. They are not unfortunate setbacks. They are instructions.

When you are living in the Belief Gap, you will be surrounded by obstacles made of doubt. Regulators will tell you your model is non-compliant. Incumbents will tell you the market doesn't want what you're selling. Customers will tell you your product is too confusing. Your own co-founders, in their darkest moments, will wonder if it's all a mistake (as you'll soon see).

If you interpret this wall of doubt as a stop sign, and many founders do, your company will stall and die. Your engine will run out of fuel right in the middle of the canyon. But if you interpret it as a directional sign—as a set of clues telling you exactly where you need to build, what you need to prove, and how you need to argue—you will move forward. The obstacle doesn't just get you to the other side; it *is* the other side, assembled piece by piece. The friction isn't a bug; it's the feature that lets you gain traction.

Remember the story from Chapter 1 of Brian Chesky and Joe Gebbia, the broke founders of Airbnb living deep inside the Belief Gap? Faced with a mountain of debt and a wall of investor doubt so high they couldn't see the top, they famously resorted to designing and selling presidential-themed breakfast cereal just to pay their rent.

When I first told you about that, I framed it as a heroic act of survival—a desperate search for "Belief fuel." Now seen through a Stoic lens, it becomes something more profound. It becomes a masterclass in metabolizing obstacles.

The obstacle wasn't just their empty bank account; it was the narrative investors had created about them: "two gritty guys with a weird idea who don't know how to execute." No amount of pitching could break through that wall of doubt. The cereal box stunt wasn't just about making $30,000; it was about rewriting the story.

The act of designing, gluing, and hustling those boxes was a direct collision with their obstacle. It reframed their narrative from "can they sell this crazy idea?"

to "look how relentlessly they act." Investor doubt didn't vanish—it was transformed. The obstacle forced them to demonstrate the very "cockroach" tenacity that Paul Graham would later bet on. They didn't go around the wall of doubt; they disassembled it and used the bricks to build their path forward. The obstacle became the way.

III.

To understand why doubt feels so uniquely paralyzing—why it can freeze a brilliant founder in their tracks—we have to go back to the basic wiring of the human brain.

As I touched on earlier, Dr. Karl Friston has shown your brain spends every millisecond of its existence creating a model of the world and then updating that model based on sensory feedback. **The reality you perceive is a "controlled hallucination," a story your brain tells itself about what's happening.**

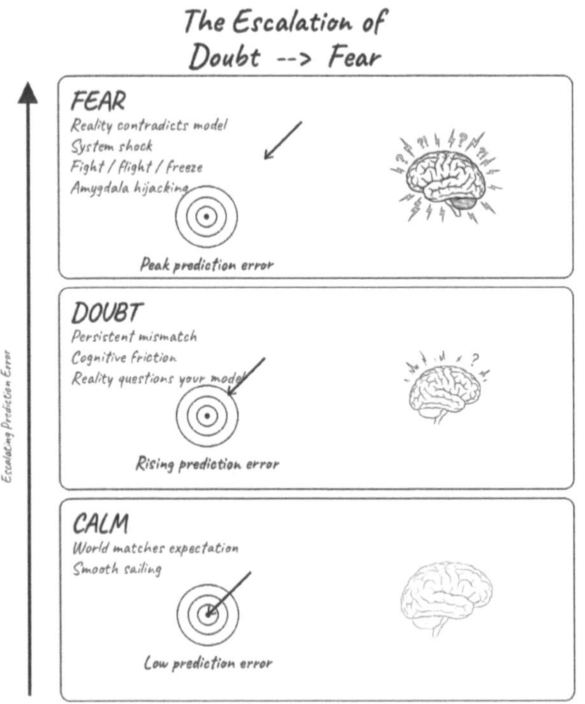

Figure 12—The impact of free Energy Shock levels on the nervous system

When the world behaves as predicted, your brain hums along efficiently. But when reality contradicts your prediction, your brain generates a jolt of what Friston calls "free energy," basically your nervous system's reaction to an unwelcome surprise. This is a prediction error, and your brain hates it. Its primary job is to minimize prediction energy shock. There is a scale of prediction error.

Doubt is the cognitive friction created by a persistent prediction error on a low or long-term level. Doubt isn't a shocking, life-threatening faulty prediction, but it's not what you were counting on. Doubt is the feeling that arises when the world's feedback—an investor's "no," a customer's complaint, a regulator's threat—continuously clashes with your internal model, with your Belief.

This is where Dr. Earl Miller's work on attention becomes so critical. Our attention system, as he describes it, can operate like a wide-angle "floodlight," taking in the entire scene, or a narrow-beam "spotlight," focusing on a single detail. When we are calm and confident, we can use our floodlight to see the whole hockey rink, to anticipate where the puck is going, to decide, consciously, what to focus on.

But when we are confronted with a powerful prediction error—with the fear and uncertainty of doubt—our ancient survival circuits kick in. The spotlight of our attention narrows dramatically (subconsciously) and locks onto the source of the threat. You stop seeing the ice. You see only the puck screaming toward your face and pray you can back-bend like Neo.

Great leadership requires that you balance your use of the spotlight vs the floodlight, but it takes awareness in the Observation phase to do that. In a startup, if you aren't aware of subconscious bias or threats this means you stop seeing the vast market opportunity and obsess over the one competitor who just raised a new round. You stop seeing the hundred customers who love your product and stare at the one angry tweet from a user who had a bad experience. You fixate on the regulator's rejection letter instead of the thousands of potential users who are still waiting for your solution. The founder's job is to have a system that consciously forces the spotlight back into a floodlight. That system is the BOODA loop, and its first rule of engagement against doubt is simple: Decide at 70%. Waiting for 100% certainty is how you surrender to fear; it is the neurological equivalent of freezing until the market passes you by. Your goal is to run an experiment to get that final 30%, not to wait for it to be delivered.

This is where the Founder's Creed and the BOODA Doctrine become your tools for metabolizing obstacles and eliminating doubt. They are a practical, repeatable system for processing the free energy of doubt and turning it into focused action.

When an obstacle appears, the loop gives you a set of instructions:

Believe: This is your anchor. Your Creed is the unwavering North Star that keeps the temporary storm of doubt from throwing you completely off course. Before you even analyze the obstacle, you remind yourself of your core mission.

I talked about turning your company to a verb, like Uber has done. It was their belief in a better transportation model that allowed them to see regulatory fights not as a reason to quit, but as a necessary part of the journey, those obstacles were their way.

Observe: Look at the obstacle with an unblinking eye. What is *really* there? Strip away the fear and emotion. A regulator's doubt isn't just an arbitrary "no." What is the real concern behind it? Often, it's a legitimate issue like public safety, insurance, or driver screening. When you observe the true nature of the obstacle, it stops being a monster and becomes a problem to be solved.

Orient: This is the crucial step of placing the obstacle on your Shared Belief Map. Does this new piece of information challenge one of your foundational Core Beliefs? Or is it simply a data point that will help you test one of your Hypotheses? For Uber, regulatory pushback didn't challenge their Core Belief that people wanted a better taxi service. It simply meant their Hypothesis about how to enter a market needed to be tested and refined. This act of Orientation turns a crisis into a learning opportunity.

Decide: Based on your Orientation, you make a choice. The key is to decide on the smallest, fastest, and cheapest action that will generate the most valuable data about the obstacle. You're not trying to solve the whole problem at once. You're trying to run an experiment. Airbnb didn't decide to "solve their funding problem." They decided to sell cereal boxes to survive another month and generate a new data point about their own tenacity.

Act: You ship the experiment. You make the move. You publish the data. You collide with the obstacle in a controlled way. This is the only way to get real-world feedback and reduce the prediction error. Ship and ask a lot of questions. Action is the antidote for the paralysis of doubt.

This loop transforms the obstacle from a passive, terrifying threat into an active, data-generating process. It's the engine that turns the bricks of doubt into the bridge of progress. But what happens when those bricks start to collapse?

IV

When I was 34 years old, my world looked like (and was) the high-flying story of a successful entrepreneur and family man. My daughter was a year old; my wife was six months pregnant with our second child, and I had just launched ODIN Technologies with talent and technology spun out of MIT's Auto-ID Lab.

We were a tight team of five, including a business school buddy—an Annapolis grad and former Navy ship driver—who I nearly considered a co-founder. We hit some choppy waters in the Belief Gap; but were motoring steadily across it. The demand for RFID from Wal-Mart and Department of Defense suppliers was a powerful tailwind.

Then we sailed head-on into a bow-breaking obstacle. And that obstacle was me.

For years, I had been living in a state of chronic fear, especially a terror of flying. This meant my body was in a constant state of low-grade panic and anxiety, a non-stop angst loop flooding my system with cortisol. I could feel the fear center - my amygdala - trying to take control of my life. It felt like a ball of tears permanently lodged in my stomach, ready to shoot up my throat at any moment and send me into an episode of child-like despair. My way of coping was a brutal routine of self-medication: Alcohol was the foundation, but other stress added to the recipe. I'd hammer myself at Gold's Gym at 5:30 a.m to try and work away the guilt and shame of drinking so much, then I'd survive a founder's full-throttle day fueled by half-dozen Diet Cokes, and then start drinking Guinness from the little dorm-room fridge sitting next to my desk, usually around six, often with the team. I was running on four hours of sleep a night, a diet of caffeine and alcohol, and pure adrenaline. It was killing me. Literally.

Not surprisingly, my body broke. I got sick. Not just a cold or flu, but a deathly, can't-lift-my-head-off-the-pillow sickness. I ended up at Johns Hopkins Hospital because no one at the local hospital could figure out why my immune system had simply vanished. This was the first wall. Then the obstacle looked insurmountable when the best doctors in the world told me that if their last-ditch treatment didn't work, I had two weeks to live. That's an obstacle. But at least I had hired a great COO to help grow ODIN to a great company...or so I thought.

We had our first major client, the US Secret Service, and proposals out to key Wal-Mart suppliers. The company was just taking off. We had money coming in, with both internal and external believers. Now, with me lying in a sterile hospital room, tubes running everywhere, the team had no one at the rudder. So I did what any founder would do: I turned to my COO, my trusted Navy officer and business school classmate, to lead.

And that's when the second, bigger wall appeared. A week into my adventure in the oncology ward at Johns Hopkins, my COO went to my wife—who was already dealing with the unimaginable stress of her husband potentially leaving her with a toddler and another baby on the way—and delivered his message. "Hey…ah, things are looking pretty tough," he said. "and I got an offer from a consulting firm at a great salary, so please tell Paddy I'm leaving."

What a great guy.

The key leader I thought would take much of my workload and start to scale up with it, and whose leadership background could really inspire the team, bailed when things got tough. He didn't even have the courage to come to me directly. Fortunately, the team had a Shared Belief Map and a clear unified direction.

I thought the obstacle of me being sick couldn't get bigger. I was wrong. Our first obstacle was a false summit of the worst kind, the departure of the second in command could have easily been the end of ODIN. What saved us wasn't a heroic leader stepping up. It was the clarity of our mission. The team knew what mattered above all else: delivering for the Secret Service, solving the physics problems of getting good reads on metal handguns. While I was fighting for my life and our COO was abandoning ship like a rat, the rest of the team—the true believers—rallied around that single, unambiguous goal. They didn't need me to micromanage them because they were already indoctrinated in the most important creed of all: do the work, deliver the result. Their Shared Belief became the rudder, and those obstacles, because how we got over them, became our way forward.

My experience in that hospital bed was as educational as a whole season of Shark Tank, I thought about what was working and what needed changing. The time reflecting helped forge a playbook for dealing with the kind of existential obstacles every founder will face.

1.   **Your First Obstacle is Often You.** The initial crisis at ODIN wasn't an RFID reader malfunction or a market shift; it was my own body and mind literally devouring itself from the inside. Founders are brilliant at managing external systems but often neglect their internal one. Your physical and mental health isn't a luxury; it's a core component of your company's infrastructure. I advise a lot of CEOs on strategy, and I always touch on exercise, diet and sleep as competitive advantages. Leading from a constant state of amygdala hijack—wired by fear, caffeine, and no sleep—isn't hustling; it's a reckless gamble.
     The lesson: Manage your own biology. Your ability to stay calm under pressure is your company's ultimate shock absorber. Wade into

uncertainty knowing you'll learn what you need to learn. Practice conscious breathing.

2. **Clarity is Your Ultimate Contingency Plan.** When I was taken out of the game, our complex strategies didn't matter. What saved the company was a simple, powerful, and universally understood mission: "Create supremely satisfied clients" and that meant deliver for the Secret Service. A crisis will burn away everything but your core purpose. *The lesson:* Make your mission and key objectives so clear that your team can execute autonomously, even if the leadership structure collapses. A clear mission is the ultimate form of empowerment.

3. **Filter for Believers, Not Resumes.** My COO had a world-class resume— Annapolis, Navy officer, Darden MBA. He was a perfect leader on paper. But under pressure, his commitment was to his salary, not the mission. The rest of the team, the ones who stayed and focused, were the true leaders. *The lesson:* An obstacle is a brutally effective filter. It reveals who is a mercenary and who is a missionary. Hire for belief in the mission above all else. A smaller team of true believers is infinitely more powerful than a larger team of talented mercenaries.

4. **Action is the Antidote to Despair.** The team didn't hold endless meetings to strategize about the company's future with a dying founder and a departing COO. They Acted on the one thing they could control: the client project. Focusing on a tangible, productive task was the antidote to the paralyzing fear and uncertainty. *The lesson:* When faced with an overwhelming obstacle, shrink the world. Identify the single most important, controllable action and execute it with ferocious focus. Momentum, no matter how small, is the cure for paralysis.

The comfortable island of the Belief Glut, where founders admire their own pitch decks and the market remains serenely indifferent, is a seductive place. It's a place free of doubt, because it's free of feedback. But the Belief Gap is where the real work happens, and doubt is the toll you pay to cross it.

Founders who win are the ones who build cultures that normalize the BOODA process. They create environments where obstacles are seen as routine, not catastrophic. MIT's famous "hack" culture does this brilliantly. Students learn, through practice, that resistance and difficulty are not signs to stop. They are signs that you're on the right track.

Your job as a founder is to build the attitude that no idea is a dead-end inside your company. You need to teach your team that when a regulator says no, when a competitor launches a new feature, or when a customer churns, it's not a crisis. It's just the next turn of the loop. More data. It's a new prompt, a new piece of information, a new instruction for the path forward. If you plant the seed that these obstacles will appear, then when they do you help reduce Free Energy in your team. The obstacles, even though previously unknown, are not a total surprise.

So, here is the creed for the canyon. Here is the doctrine for the doubt.

Belief without obstacles is just a hallucination. It's the easy, untested conviction of the Belief Glut.

Obstacles without Belief are just paralysis. It's a long list of reasons why nothing can be done.

Belief, plus an obstacle, plus the BOODA loop—is the formula for momentum.

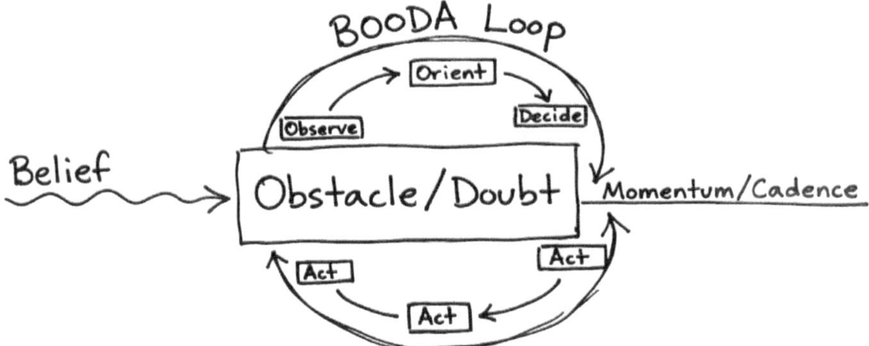

Figure 13—Action is the foundation of momentum when facing an obstacle

When the world doubts you, when the walls seem too high and the canyon too wide, remember the stories of Virta, of Airbnb, of Uber, of ODIN. Remember the quiet wisdom of a Roman emperor. The obstacle is not a detour from your path. It *is* the path. It is the raw material from which you will build your bridge to the other side. Don't avoid it. Don't bemoan it. Use it.

Metabolizing obstacles is more of the work. It's the grinding, day-to-day process of turning friction into fuel. But as you navigate the canyon, another, more subtle question begins to emerge: *Is it working?* How do you sustain the high-octane Belief required for this fight—not just in yourself, but in your team, your investors, and your first brave customers? Shouting the creed from your side of the gap isn't enough. You have to send proof. You have to ship.

This was the challenge now facing the team at MedXit. They had their Shared Belief Map. They had their rules of engagement and were learning to cycle through BOODA with a new, disciplined speed. They had even stared down their own internal obstacles and come out stronger. But to win over the US healthcare establishment, to turn skeptical doctors into allies and cautious hospital administrators into partners, they needed more than a powerful Belief. They needed to make their progress undeniable. They had to prove that their mission to "empower longer health-span through accessible data" wasn't just a noble slogan, but an outcome they could produce and, more importantly, an outcome they could measure.

How do you measure something as seemingly intangible as "empowerment" or "health-span" or what I called earlier "hygiene?" How do you convince a world that runs on spreadsheets and clinical trials when your greatest asset is a Belief?

You do it by finding a way to measure the unmeasurable. You do it by taking the invisible shockwaves your company is creating and giving them color, shape, and weight. You do it by turning your conviction into a case built on irrefutable data. To cross their own Belief Gap, the founders in Kendall Square needed to do for patient wellness what a young determined English nurse once did for soldier mortality in the filth of a Crimean War hospital: they needed to make the color of their belief visible for all to see.

6

The Color of Belief

I.

A young nurse named Florence Nightengale was standing next to the gated entrance of a military hospital, her face turned into the wind, yet she couldn't escape the smell of rot. The Barrack Hospital stood heavy on the hill on the Asian side of what was then called Constantinople, now Turkey. From a distance the hospital looked all stone and shadow. Inside, the wards were long and dark, the air thick with the grotesque mixed aromas of gangrene, smoke, sweat, and the sour stench of infected wounds eating away at flesh. Men lay on the floor when the cots were filled, their boots still on, their uniforms stiff with blood and filth.

Florence had come here with 38 nurses that she trained under the same rigorous discipline as the German nursing school that trained her. At the time a new theory of disease was developing, an idea known as miasma theory, which posited that diseases were spread by "bad air" from decomposing organic matter[1]. The gag-inducing air filling her nose and mouth were all the data she needed to know the place was, as soldiers called it, a death factory. The challenge she had, 175

---

1   Frank M. Snowden, *Epidemics and Society: From the Black Death to the Present* (New Haven: Yale University Press, 2019), 51–75.

years before MedXit even existed, was how to measure the unmeasurable. She had to collect enough data to prove that better hygiene could save lives. I believe in the metaphor of operational hygiene as you've seen but Florence lived and breathed by the literal adoption of hygiene to kill germs and to save soldier's lives.

The whole British Army knew the death factory by reputation. They called it Scutari in low voices like a curse, after the town in Turkey where it was built, the site of a former cesspool. To be sent there was to be sent to death's waiting room. Scutari swallowed men whole, and few came out alive.

Florence Nightingale came to this horrible British Army base with a belief, a conviction so radical for its time that it was seen as quaint or even foolish. She believed that the biggest killer in war wasn't the enemy's cannons, but the army's own filth. She believed in the power of soap. The senior officers dismissed her ideas as a girl's fancy, a crazy notion the fairer sex did not have the capability to truly understand. Soon they would learn a lesson in humility from that girl.

The doctors, constantly overworked, were annoyed by this young woman with the strong voice and even stronger conviction. To the soldiers she was a foolish kid with strange ideas about hygiene. Soldiers saw death as a consequence of war. What created even more obstacles inside her Belief Gap was the fact that all the men in charge viewed women as supplicants to do the menial tasks, not to tell them secrets of the world. Certainly not to have the audacity to advise them on any part of fighting a war. Yet she knew the truth couldn't be denied - for every one soldier who died from a wound on the battlefield, seven died in the hospital from disease. It was a death factory, operated by the very people sworn to save lives.

Nightingale, however, saw something else. She saw a system that was killing its own men through sheer, bloody ignorance and arrogance. She had a rock-solid Belief that lives could be spared with a few simple actions. But how could she prove it? How could she convince the stiff-lipped, know-it-all generals and politicians back in London that her belief was not just a woman's intuition, but the foundation of a strategic imperative that would help the Ottoman side win the war and stop the brutal Russian aggression? How could she get them to cross that Belief Gap?

As a woman living in the 19th Century no matter how passionate she was about something, without proof, her opinion would be dismissed as imagination. She couldn't just tell them to "believe in cleanliness." She had to make them see what she saw during her time at Scutari. She had to measure the unmeasurable.

So, in between her 20-hour shifts tending to the dying, Nightingale became what we would today call a data scientist. She began to count. She meticulously recorded the cause of death for every single soldier. She tracked mortality rates, correlated them with sanitary conditions, and compiled vast tables of statistics. She and her team of 38 nurses, first had to procure 200 Turkish towels, clean shirts, soap, and scrubbing brushes. Then, they set to work. They scrubbed the floors, cleaned the laundry, and insisted on basic sanitation. She was the Billy Beane[2] of the Crimean war - she cared less about popular opinion, accepted methods, or unproven superstitions and only tracked data-driven results. She was a statistics junkie with OCD, a quant jock with a mission.

In the 1800s, just like today, tables of numbers were usually a cure for insomnia. A spreadsheet (or for Flo, a ledger page) will never change the minds of highly confident Generals or Admirals. So she invented a new way to show her data by telling a story. She created a chart, a beautiful and terrifying diagram she called the "coxcomb" or "polar area diagram." It was a circle broken into a spiral of colored wedges, where each wedge represented a month of the war. The size of the wedge represented the number of deaths. And the color of the wedge represented the cause. Blue was for "preventable diseases," red was for "wounds," and black was for "all other causes."

---

2   Billy Beane was the manager of the Oakland A's who famously used data to choose his baseball players rather than traditional scouts. He became the protagonist in Michael Lewis's blockbuster book Money Ball which was later turned into a major motion picture starring Brad Pitt.

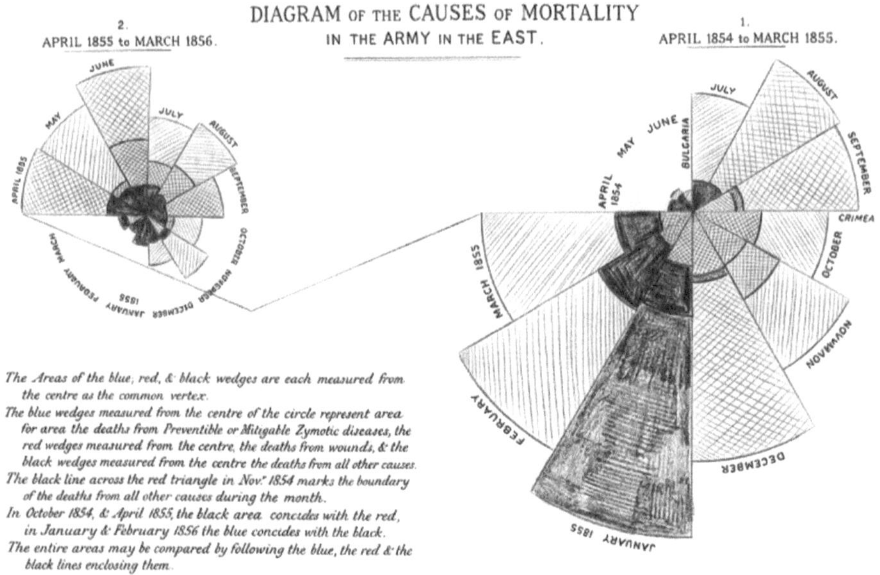

Figure 14—Statistics presented in a way that leaves no doubt of
Nightengale's belief.

The effect was instantaneous and devastating. At a glance, anyone, from
a Queen's minister to a common soldier, could see the horrifying truth. The vast
majority of the wedges were the light blue that signified death by disease. The
British Army was being defeated not by Russian bullets, but by cholera, dysentery,
and typhus. Her belief was no longer an opinion; it was a mathematical certainty,
rendered in color. Florence created a Shared Belief Map that changed the entire
future of nursing. Like all the startups that I've helped implement the BOODA
Doctrine, she created a system to show her conclusion and prove a hypothesis.
She, alone, owned the job of proving her hypothesis was fact, it was a Core Belief
now. Every month she'd tally the numbers and every month she would get more
and more confident in her beliefs. When a year's worth of data was there for the
world to see it went from a hypothesis to a Core Belief that cleanliness saved lives.
Soap was a savior.

Nightingale's diagram was right on target. It became an arrow in her political
quiver, a tool she used to shame the government into action. It led to a complete
overhaul of the military healthcare system and saved countless lives. She had done

the impossible. She had measured the impact of a belief and it eventually took the death toll from 40% of all soldiers admitted to the hospital down to 2%.

Many founders face similar challenges of how to measure results. After you've forged your creed, built your map, and started building your team, you are left with the same question that haunted Florence Nightingale: Is our system working? How do you prove, not just to your investors but to yourself, that your Belief is changing the world? For the skeptics in the room, for the CFOs and the engineers who live by the mantra "what gets measured gets managed," this chapter is for you. While you can't put Belief under a microscope, you can absolutely measure the shockwaves it creates in the real world. There are the three gauges to measure the impact on your collective fuel tank.

The first place to look for evidence is in the very stem of your company's brain: your Shared Belief Map. The SBM is more than just a values statement; it's a living snapshot of your collective mind and focus. The three components to the SBM—the Core Beliefs, the Hypotheses, and the Garage—are where you need to anchor your collective observations. If you're looking for a statistical way of measuring effectiveness and direction, then the most important metric on that map is the ratio of your Core Beliefs to your Hypotheses.

Think of it as the ratio of conviction to curiosity. Simply put, it's Belief to Doubt.

A conviction unchecked by curiosity turns into the Belief Glut—the dark side of a founder's confidence. The spectacular collapse of the first global satellite phone provider serves as a harsh example of what happens when a company evolves with a fixed mindset.

Iridium set out in the 1990s to build a global satellite phone network, spending over $5 billion on a technological marvel. Their Core Belief, held with absolute certainty, was that the global market for satellite phones was enormous. Their conviction was absolute. If you measured them on the Belief framework you saw earlier, their Internal Belief score was a 10. They all Believed, however their External validation from customers and analysts was 1—maybe even 0.

But their fixed mindset drove a Belief that was not only rigid, but lacking the key principles of the BOODA Doctrine - Observation and Orientation which you'll see later. They exemplified the core flaw of the fixed mindset: they perceived their key assumptions as static and unchangeable. They failed to treat a critical assumption as a testable hypothesis: would anyone actually want a clunky, expensive satellite phone in a world where cellular phones were rapidly becoming cheaper and better? It was similar to the first mistakes MedExit made about treating a Hypothesis as a Core Belief; the billion-dollar difference was that Iridium had no Doctrine to put a spotlight on their fatal flaw.

They did not cycle through the BOODA loop and thus ignored key market feedback. They refused to do market research or consider cheaper, alternative architectures. There was scant curiosity, no doubt, and consequently, a catastrophic Belief Glut. They didn't just Believe; they calcified. By treating a market prediction as an unchangeable 'Core Belief' rather than a 'Hypothesis' to be tested weekly, they effectively welded their BOODA loop shut.

Iridium was achingly slow to Observe the reality of the market and failed to Orient itself to the new truth of mobile connectivity. The result was one of the most spectacular bankruptcies in history, caused not by fraud, but by a fixed mindset, incompetence and the lack of an agile Doctrine that could challenge their convictions.

In contrast, companies with a growth mindset, like Netflix, constantly thrived. Netflix's Core Belief was simple: a massive market existed for unlimited entertainment. But they never let that conviction become a fixed dogma.

Instead, they constantly created Hypotheses that needed to be tested and verified every week. They constantly tested concepts, like whether binge-watching would become a cultural phenomenon or if people would pay for streaming services. When they observed major failures, like the outrage over the Qwickster spin-out, they didn't think they were right; they observed the changes and acted, using the feedback to drive the next loop.

The lessons converge on one crucial point: a fixed mindset can lead to spectacular failures, while a growth mindset fosters resilience and success. Success hinges on being willing to question your beliefs and grow with the data.

A company with a healthy belief system has a strong, stable foundation of shared Core Beliefs. These are your handful of non-negotiable truths upon which your entire enterprise is built. For the Marines, it's "We are the most elite fighting force on the planet". For MedXit, a core belief was that the Massachusetts Health and Human Services program would have 300,000 citizens on an electronic healthcare monitoring system in two years. These beliefs are the bedrock, the facts that allow the team to take risks.

But a company that is only Core Beliefs is a cult. It is dogmatic, rigid, and brittle. It is a company with a fixed mindset. Even worse, it can be built on facts designed to limit risk or exposure, consequently limiting the chance of beating competitors by taking a risk. They move slowly through the BOODA loop because they don't see any change in those Core Beliefs—they don't want to test things. With fixed Core Beliefs only, there is no room for doubt, no mechanism for learning. Founders with no Hypothesis are building a company that is convinced it has all the answers, which is the fastest way to become irrelevant and a guaranteed way of missing out on hypergrowth.

On the other side of the ledger should be your Hypotheses. These are the engines of your curiosity and the root of your competitiveness. They are the explicit acknowledgment of what you don't know but think could be true. They are the missions you send your team on to explore - the unknown territory of your market. A company with a healthy number of hypotheses is a company that is constantly learning, constantly adapting, constantly stress-testing its own assumptions. Go back to MedXit—their Core Belief was that the Mass government wanted 300,000 patients on an electronic healthcare system. This didn't need to be tested and didn't need an owner to verify because this was brought forward as a fact from the Department of Health and Human Services. The *Hypothesis* was that MedXit could get 20% market share in two years, 60,000 patients. That hypothesis needed to be tested every week—did we sign up more people, are folks finding an alternative, what are competitors spending their time on? All crucial questions that need thoughtful and very fast answers. Decide and Act.

Compared to the fixed mindset of "only Core Beliefs," a company that is "only Hypotheses" is a fast moving ship spinning in circles. It is in a state of constant, aimless pivoting. It has no core conviction, no North Star to guide its explorations. This is the fate of countless startups that chase every new trend, pivoting from a social media app for dogs one month to a blockchain-based coffee subscription the next. They are so busy testing every possible idea that they never build a real identity. They are a company that is so open-minded that its brain has fallen out. When I started ODIN I had two strong Core Beliefs. Walmart, the largest retailer in the world had announced a mandate that every supplier would have to put RFID tags (using a new standard called the Electronic Product Code (EPC) on every box that was shipped to them. Walmart has 10,000 suppliers. So our anchoring core belief was that 10,000 customers exists for our solution. Our hypothesis was that we could get 20% market share. We also knew that the US Department of

Defense was going to put out a $75 million contract—so another Core Belief that didn't need to be tested. We also believed we could own the "physics" of RFID in our marketing and reputation—this was another hypothesis. So, like MedXit, we had 3-4 core beliefs and 4-5 hypothesis to test.

The health of your creed is reflected in the balance you as a team strike when trying to close the Belief Gap. You need enough Core Beliefs to provide a stable identity, and enough Hypotheses to drive progress and help you win and keep cycling through your BOODA Loops. This ratio of Core Beliefs to Hypotheses is your first tangible measurement. Is it close to balanced? Is it changing over time? Are you successfully converting your Hypotheses into new Core Beliefs as you learn? Are you occasionally taking items out of the Garage to test as a new Hypothesis when you see another Hypothesis isn't going to be true? Or are your Core Beliefs being invalidated, forcing you to go back to the drawing board?

The SBM is not just a map; it's a diagnostic tool. It's the blueprint that shows you the structural integrity of your Shared Beliefs. Aim for 2-3 Core Beliefs and 3-4 Hypotheses that you constantly probe and test. For hyper-growth companies you want the scales tipped 60-65% in favor of Hypothesis you are constantly testing and validating. That means you are gathering more data than your competitors—that's a strategic advantage.

In the early days of the Internet, there was a fierce, winner-take-all battle for the soul of online search. In one corner, you had a host of established, well-funded players: AOL, Yahoo, AltaVista, Lycos. They were the incumbents, the big, powerful armies with all the resources. In the other corner, you had two graduate students in a Stanford dorm room with a funny name that had something to do with big numbers: Google. By the time these two guys got their search engine launched they were the 15th entrant in the market. So much for all those investors who bet on a first-mover advantage.

On paper, it was no contest. But Google had a secret weapon. It wasn't just their superior search algorithm. It was their speed and their Belief.

In his book, *In The Plex*, Steven Levy tells the story of Google's early engineering culture.[3] It was a culture obsessed, to a degree that seemed almost insane, with the speed of its BOODA loop. While their competitors were having endless meetings to debate strategy, Google was running thousands of small experiments

---

3　　　Steven Levy, In the Plex: How Google Thinks, Works, and Shapes Our Lives Pages 80-92 (New York: Simon & Schuster, 2011).

every day. They had a system that allowed any engineer to test a new idea on a small fraction of live traffic, get real-time data, and make a decision in hours, not months. They were discovering data their competitors didn't have. They were winning because they were looping. They were winning because they Believed the data they generated could tell a story.

Their Decision-Making Principles were simple and brutal, two seemed to stand above all others: data wins and the users comes first. Their Shared Belief was that the best way to build a great product was to test everything. They had built a machine for learning, a corporate brain that could cycle through their loop at a dizzying pace. Want to know if you get more clicks on an ad in the upper left or lower right. Run the two ads on 1,500 people one upper left the other lower right then see who gets the most clicks. 20 minutes maximum, and voila! More data, more information, more motivation to go do another test. They would gather more data their competitors didn't have. They also believed that paying to get higher in ad rankings was cheating the end-user of ideal information, it went against user-first Principle. They searched for the best way to get relevant results, and they created back-link weighting, and key phrase algorithms that were in service of the user, not the advertisers.

This is the second, and perhaps most critical, measurement of your creed: the speed of your BOODA loop. How long does it take for your team to go from a new observation to a committed action? Is it hours, or is it months? How long before they convert a Hypothesis into a Core Belief, or kill it as a non-truth?

A slow feedback loop isn't just a problem; it's a fatal diagnosis for a company striving for hyper-growth. It signals a weak, misaligned belief system and a culture choking on politics or indecision. It's the sound of stagnation. It's kind of what it feels like inside a behemoth government contractor like Lockheed Martin or General Dynamics. It sounds like this: "We'll have to wait. It's August. Nothing happens in August. So let's plan on September, but not the first weeks of September because everyone is digging out." Suddenly you're months away from action.

This is an organization grinding its cylinders—all noise, no momentum. No growth engine anymore. It's burning fuel not to advance, but to create friction and fight itself.

Blockbuster Video burned tankers of fuel without moving. They were the fixed-mindset Goliath to Netflix's growth-mindset David. When Netflix's CEO

Reed Hastings—the man obsessed with hiring "Fighter Pilots"—flew to Dallas with a brilliant proposal for Blockbuster, he was met with contempt. His offer: Buy Netflix and they will handle the online presence for Blockbuster, essentially white-labeling Netflix, and Blockbuster in turn focuses on their stores.

The response from Blockbuster's CEO? Laughter.

Blockbuster's loop for observing and orienting to a threat was measured in months, maybe years. They believed people wanted to go into a store and get a DVD because that's how it's been done for years. Netflix's loop was measured in days maybe hours. By the time Blockbuster realized the world had changed, Netflix was already running it. Blockbuster filed for bankruptcy in 2010.

A fast loop, on the other hand, is the sound of a high-performance culture. It's the sign of a team that has a strong, agreed, predictive model (their SBM) and a clear set of rules for how to update it (their decision-making principles). They don't waste time or energy on repetitive arguments. They have a shared understanding of what they Believe, which allows them to focus all their energy on what they need to learn. You already know one of the most famous hyper-growth phrases, it focuses on BOODA-like speed; Facebook's creed—*Move fast and break things*. That was one of their values; they celebrated well intentioned failures. They only hired people ready to take risks and hang on to their conviction. They lived inside the BOODA loop.

You can, and should, literally measure the speed of your loops. Pick a recent, significant decision your team made. How many meetings did it take? How many people had to sign off? How many days passed between the initial observation and the final action? And critically how many days before you got new data and started to go through the whole end-to-end process again? That number is the beats-per-minute of your company's heart. It's a hard, quantitative metric that tells you more about the health of your culture than any employee satisfaction survey ever could. It's a great thing to do for each of your 4-5 hypothesis. You should be testing those out weekly.

If we go back to MedXit, their hypothesis is that they can sign up 60,000 users during a two year period. Now they are trying to figure out ways to do that. Let's say they want to allocate $50,000 to ads this month to recruit new patients. The clock starts ticking when that decision is made. How many users are on now? Let's say 500. They all agreed on budget of $50,000 for one month. What does the ad copy say? Is Gio going to win or Sandra? How many variants do you want? What are the buying personas they are going after? Decisions and then Action. How long does it take for the first ad(s) to go live? What are the results after the first week? Get around that loop again with the new data you observed. Speed is much more important than perfection for a hypergrowth company, because speed gets you more data and more data clarify your target and the trajectory getting there. But for their company to truly thrive at hyper-growth speed, the energy generated by these rapid cycles must create more than just data points and new users. That energy needs to create a signal that travels far beyond a simple advertisement, and most importantly that must be shaped and shared before entropy creeps in and kill the momentum of the company. Because doubt is really the acceleration of entropy, energy breaking down, heat cooling off, light dimming down. Company dying. So how can you measure whether or not you are getting across the Belief Gap and not stuck in the Glut?

The final gauge is the most subtle, but also the most powerful. It's the measure of your creed's magnetism. A strong Belief system doesn't just exist inside the walls of your company; it radiates outward. It sends a clear, powerful signal into the world. The question is, what kind of echo does it create?

Belief is measured by who you attract and who you repel.

Think back to the Netflix Culture Deck. It was a 125-slide cultural magnet, designed with a specific polarity. It was built to attract a very particular kind of person—the "fighter pilot," the high-performer who craved freedom and responsibility and was comfortable with brutal honesty. And it was explicitly designed to repel everyone else. It was a filter, and its effectiveness was the ultimate measure of their creed.

The target of the company can be completely different than what Netflix or MedXit were trying to achieve. Take a company like Patagonia, for example. Their founder, Yvon Chouinard, built his company around a different, but equally powerful mission: that a business can be a tool for environmental salvation. His core belief was "The pitons[4] my friends and I are using are damaging the rock and aren't reusable. We desperately need a better solution." He knew the problem to be a fact because he was suffering that problem every time he went up a rock face. This idea of building something that will last a lifetime, of building the highest quality possible is what led to their famous "Don't Buy This Jacket" ad campaign

---

4   A piton is a flat spike the size of two fingers with a hole in one end. The piton is pounded into rock cracks to anchor a climber's rope. They are left behind in the rock when the climber finishes the route.

in 2011 mocking fashionistas. The clear message; Patagonia clothing wasn't for those looking for the new collection every year. The ad was a cultural magnet of its own. It was a signal that repelled consumers looking for disposable fashion, and powerfully attracted customers and employees who shared Chouinard's Belief in sustainability and anti-consumerism. Both Netflix and Patagonia have incredibly strong cultures, but they have different polarities. They both measure their Belief by the quality of the tribe they attract, one focuses on employees the other focuses on the environment.

Your company is sending out a signal right now. What is it?

The signal is in your job descriptions, in your interview process, in the stories your employees tell their friends and of course across any form of communication from X to TikTok. Is that signal clear? Is it attracting the right people? Is it aligned with your principles and values or is it regurgitating Enron, leaving you sounding like you're circling the drain. It's your job to lead your team across the Belief Gap, to make sure that your signal is exactly on target, and the echo coming back is just what you put out, so listen carefully to that echo.

Like Florence found, things aren't always easy to measure; but the data is there, if you know how to look for it. What is your offer acceptance rate for top candidates? Are you losing them to bigger companies with higher salaries, or are they turning down more money to join your mission? What is your employee retention rate? Are your best people, your true believers, staying for the long haul, or are they the first ones out the door when things get tough? What are your internal promotion rates, and are you only promoting people who are rock-stars in their current roles? During your 360 degree quarterly reviews you should encourage every employee to ask their direct supervisor—"If I got an offer from Competitor A today, would you fight to keep me?" If the answer is "no" both people should do something to act on that information. If the answer is "Yes" then a raise and some more responsibility are in order.

But the most powerful echo of all is the one we hear beyond our walls in the long term. It's how much energy your creed radiates with others. The ultimate proof that our Belief system at ODIN was working didn't come because we won a contract, or because our employees were fulfilled and happy. The proof came because our Belief was so infectious it helped inspire others outside our company to take the leap and become founders themselves. ODIN's influence created at least a dozen new companies from our employees to our client's employees who were inspired by our Belief. It was an echo of our creed, helping to create new founders in the world. Certainly, Netflix and Patagonia have also inspired dozens, probably hundreds, to be founders and create their own creed, it's the sign of a true winner. Helping others succeed always echoes back to you with more success.

The echo is the final, and perhaps most profound, way to measure your Belief. Does it inspire belief in others? Does it give them the courage to start their own journey? Can your Belief help others overcome the doubt they'll face around every corner of an entrepreneurial journey? A truly powerful creed doesn't just build a company. It builds more founders. One of the things I am most proud of in my very long and successful career was that five of my direct reports went on to become CEOs in their own right, and one of my direct reports went on to run AI for Amazon. My Belief in our team and our ability to do the impossible or the unimaginable rubbed off on the men and women I spent most of my time with. Teaching them the BOODA Doctrine gave them a very effective tool to win in their own markets and scale at hyper speed, learning with them helped me become a better leader.

II.

Florence Nightingale returned to Britain from the Crimea War a hero. Her reputation for saving lives and changing medicine was worthy of a Nobel Prize if it had been created, but that would come a few decades later. However, she wasn't satisfied. She knew that her work was not just about winning a single battle against filth in one hospital. It was about changing the entire belief system of the British establishment.

The data kept driving her. Like Billy Bean coming into the play-offs, she continued her work of measurement. She used her newfound fame and her powerful data to lobby for sweeping public health reforms. Her work led to the creation of the first professional nursing school, the establishment of sanitation standards for hospitals, and a fundamental shift in how the world thought about the connection between hygiene and health. And at a time when women didn't have the right to vote and were thought of as second-class citizens, she created a newfound respect and appreciation for nurses at hospitals across the globe.

The ultimate measure of her belief was not in the charts she created, but in the world she changed. It was in the millions of lives saved by a simple, powerful idea that, before her, had been dismissed as nonsense.

Is your company leaving a dent in the universe? Are you changing your industry, or creating a whole new one? Did you at least create a new category? Did you build something that will outlast you? Did you help pay for new babies, new houses and college tuitions by creating wealth for your employees? Did you, like Nightingale, take a Belief that the world saw as foolish and turn it into the new common sense?

Impact is the only measurement that truly matters in the end. It is the final, unblinking judgment of the Founder's Creed.

You've just crossed the first threshold: from private conviction to a shared creed.

In Part I you learned to name and navigate the Belief Gap—that lonely stretch between "this will never work" and "this will change everything." You saw how founders like the Airbnb trio, and the MedXit team transformed doubt into evidence and faith into alignment.

Through the Shared Belief Map, you distilled raw conviction into refined fuel. You learn now speaks one language, anchored in core beliefs and hypotheses you can test. You've built the refinery. But a refinery without combustion is just storage.
Now the question shifts: How do you turn shared belief into coordinated speed?

The next part reveals how belief enters motion—through the **BOODA Loop:**

Believe → Observe → Orient → Decide → Act.

This is where founders become commanders. Where conviction turns into clarity, and clarity into conquest.

Strap in—the loop spins fast.

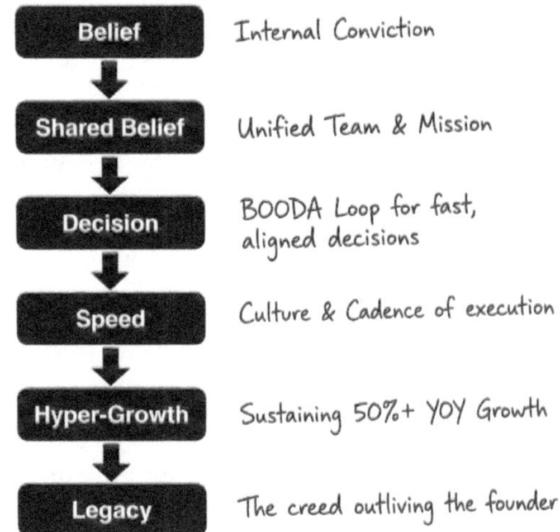

From Belief to Battle: The Inner Game

I.

The Shared Belief Map hung on the wall of MedXit's Cambridge office like a constitution for a new country, a declaration signed in the ink of hard-won alignment. This was their creed for hyper-growth. The energy in the room was transformed from just a couple months ago. The low-grade friction that had been slowing them down for much of the year—Sandra's clinical caution grinding against Giovanni's aggressive growth-hacking—was gone. In its place was the clean, quiet hum of a machine whose parts finally moved in concert. They had done the hard, introspective work of Part I. They had forged their Creed. But clarity is not the same as conquest.

A map lays out the journey, it is not the journey. The MedXit team could sense a new kind of tension that was both thrilling and terrifying—like the starting gun at the Olympic finals. They possessed a powerful, refined fuel source. Now, they had to build the engine—and learn to pilot it through storms—that could turn that fuel into ferocious, sustained momentum. Knowing your destination and knowing how to navigate the treacherous, unpredictable terrain to get there are two entirely different skills.

This chapter is the bridge between the two parts of this book. In Part I, we did the work of the strategist, the philosopher, the founder as visionary. We excavated our beliefs, gave them names, and forged them into a shared Creed. We built the unshakable 'B' that comes before everything.

In Part II we will do the work of the fighter pilot, the operator, the founder as commander. We will learn the disciplined, high-speed rhythm of the BOODA loop—the doctrine that turns Belief into a weapon for conquering your market. And we will practice it over and over again until the loops become muscle memory, until speed becomes blinding.

Before we can step into that cockpit, we have to acknowledge the enemy that lives not in the market, but inside our own minds. The Belief Gap doesn't just exist between you and your investors or you and potential customers; it exists between your best intentions and your flawed, brilliant, predictably irrational human brain. There's neuroscience deep at work here. I experienced this for most of what I consider my first life (before Leukemia). For years, my own default setting was fight. I saw the world as a series of obstacles to be beaten, not obstacles put there to show me the way, they were opponents to be crushed. I kept trying to run away from them or demolish them and I wasn't learning "the way." Because I kept using the same stubborn approach, the obstacles kept trying to teach me the same painful lessons. My go-to tactic was to get ready to fight with the knowledge nothing would ever be easy. That was a worldview that served me in some arenas and nearly destroyed me in others. It was a bias I couldn't see until it was almost too late.

To win the external battle, you have to first master this inner game.

Our biases aren't a character flaw; they're just the factory settings of our human operating system. Think of them as ancient, high-speed shortcuts designed to save cognitive energy and keep us from being eaten by Saber-tooth tigers. We're hardwired for self-preservation—led by the amygdala, a tiny, almond-shaped relic that was once our best friend in the savannah but has become a liability in the boardroom. In our modern world, this fear center is essentially running two-million-year-old software on a high-stakes hardware loop that desperately needs an update.

When you drop that primitive wiring into the high-uncertainty, high-pressure environment of a startup, it doesn't produce logic; it produces panic and anxiety. It triggers a survival response that forces most founders to fight, freeze or flee—often right off a cliff—while in my case, it just made me want to fight. The BOODA Doctrine is your defense system against these evolutionary malfunctions, but to win, you first have to recognize the specific "pack of beasts" that is currently sabotaging your brain. I've looked at the data, and I think there are four primary mindsets standing in the way of founder success. Do you see yourself in the chameleon, the ant, the donkey or the gorilla?

The first is our confirmation bias chameleon. This creature is a master of disguise, its skin perfectly matching the color of your existing beliefs. It whispers in your ear that the glowing feedback from three friendly customers is a definitive market trend, while the critical data from thirty anonymous users is just statistical noise from people who "don't get it." At my experiential marketing startup, dwinQ, we were mesmerized by this chameleon. We became obsessed with a technically brilliant "wow" feature that was, by all objective measures, a usability nightmare. But we loved it. It was our cleverest bit of code. So, when users in testing sessions repeatedly failed to understand it, we didn't question the feature; we questioned the users. "They're not our target audience," we'd say. "This is for sophisticated marketers." Our biases confirmed we were right in our mind. But to the market, we were wrong. We were listening to a chameleon, observing only the data that confirmed our elegant belief, and we wasted six months of runway and a quarter-million dollars building for an audience that existed only in our own minds. Your biases are what make the Orientation part of the loop a potential weakness, so find people with different biases than you and get them in your loop.

There's also that beast of agreement, the ant, the yes-man or yes-woman that doesn't speak up and challenge, just praises wonderfully. This beast can ruin your big-picture strategy meeting. You believe everyone is seeing the same destination and the same road to get there. The ant wants to do what keeps the pack moving together so she thrives on polite nods, jargon, and the shared vocabulary of your pitch deck. Everyone agrees you're going to "revolutionize the industry," but the mirage hides the fact that the engineer's revolution involves a two-year platform rebuild, while the salesperson's involves a feature they can sell tomorrow. The Shared Belief Map is the tool that makes this mirage evaporate, forcing everyone to point to the same, real oasis on the map. But the ant has to be replaced by a healthy challenger.

The donkey is that stubborn beast that exemplifies the old saying "putting good money after bad" because it feeds on a founder's grit and turns it into poison. It's the voice that says, *"We've already invested so much time/money/energy into this, we can't change direction now."* It makes you double down on a failing strategy not because you believe it will work, but because you can't bear to admit the initial investment was a loss. It's what kept the leadership at MedXit sticking to their original strategy of visiting patients in their home to give them shots or IVs for the second year of their existence. To abandon it felt like abandoning their very identity, it's where they were born. So they kept polishing a beautiful, obsolete stone while the rest of the world moved on, sinking deeper into the stink of a losing market with every visit to someone's home, until they finally trusted the data, pivoted, and found their hyper-growth path.

The last beast for me is personal. For a long time, it was my primary companion. It was a 500 pound gorilla pounding its chest in the face of every challenge, turning every negotiation into a battle, every piece of feedback into an attack, it was me against the World. It sees enemies where there could be allies and conspiracies where there was only incompetence. For much of my early life, this was my operating system. As the son of a first-generation immigrant, I was taught to never show feelings and never back down. No matter how terrified I was of life, I couldn't show weakness. I had a bad-boy reputation and a chip on my shoulder, an attitude that culminated one afternoon at the Olympic Training Center in Occoquan, Virginia. This was the spot the Head Coach of the US Rowing team picked for us Olympic hopefuls to train. I was one of 12 athletes invited there. I was training with an intensity that bordered on rage every day. I was living with my girlfriend at the time and one of the other rowers tried to hit on her, and he was talking shit about me behind my back. When it happened, my internal gorilla saw it not as a minor annoyance, but as a challenge to my entire existence. I saw red. I started a fight. Not really a fight, I hit him once and it was over. It wasn't a discussion; it was a physical altercation that got me promptly and justifiably kicked out of the training center by the woman running US Rowing. My Olympic dream, the very thing I'd been fighting for, was now even more difficult than it had to be because of my need to fight for everything. I didn't see it then, but the real opponent wasn't the guy in the fight; it was the gorilla in my own head.

Figure 15—Many Founders, like me, think they had to fight for everything. You don't and it's no fun to always be fighting.

II.

My gorilla stayed with me for years, a silent co-founder in my early ventures. It made me a relentless negotiator and a tireless competitor, but it also made me see threats everywhere. It was exhausting. The shift to tranquility began when I started working with Diana Chapman who created the 15 Commitments. Over several years of hard, uncomfortable inner work, she helped me see that the world wasn't a battlefield; it was a mirror. The hostility I perceived reflected the frequency I was broadcasting. Before long when something went sideways I wasn't raging at the world or the protagonist—I had my emotions in a healthy state that separated them from my work. It was only data.

This brings me to one of the most misunderstood scenes in cinema, from *The Godfather.* After Sonny Corleone gets ambushed and killed, the heads of the

Five Families meet to broker a peace. His brother Michael, now the heir apparent, sits silently while his father, Vito, makes a promise he has no intention of keeping. Later, when Vito is planning his revenge for Sonny's death, he explains his cold, calculated approach. "It's not personal" he famously said. "It's strictly business." The truth is not about emotion or feelings.

Most people see this as the moment Michael becomes a cold-blooded monster. But from a strategic perspective, it's the moment he masters his inner game. He detaches from the hot-headed, amygdala-driven need for immediate, passionate revenge that got his brother Sonny killed. He stops fighting the gorilla. He begins to see the world not as a series of personal insults to be avenged, but as a system to be understood and navigated. He starts to Observe and Orient before he Decides and Acts. No emotion, just data and action.

My journey wasn't about becoming a mafia don, but it was about a similar shift in perception. Through my work with Diana, I realized the world could be a very friendly place if I let it. The vibe I was sending out—one of defensiveness, of expecting a fight—was creating the very reality I claimed to despise. I was learning to adjust my perception of life from a constant fight to a potential gift. This doesn't mean you become a pushover. It means you stop wasting energy fighting ghosts. You save your strength for the real battles, and you recognize that most of what you perceive as a threat is just a misinterpretation of the data. The funny thing is, I started to notice similar attitudes (without awareness) in other people I was working with. Awareness is key. It's a shift from being a reactor to being an architect of your reality.

III.

In Chapter 6, we looked at Iridium through the cold lens of measurement—a perfect '10' on internal conviction and a '1' on external validation. But numbers only tell you *the coordinates of* a plane crash; they don't tell you the mindset of the pilot who flew it into the mountain. To understand why Iridium ignored the seemingly obvious rise of cellular technology, we have to look at the 'Inner Gorilla' running their cockpit. This wasn't a failure of math; it was a failure of the inner game.

To see what happens when an entire company is run by a gorilla—when a flawed, aggressive Belief corrupts the whole action loop (or entirely eliminates the loop) let's dive deeper into the spectacular flameout of Iridium. Iridium wasn't just a company; it was a technological Sistine Chapel conceived in a state of supreme arrogance. In the 1990s, they set out to build a constellation of 66 satellites to provide phone service to every square inch of the planet. Elon Musk was 19 years old at the time and probably never dreamed of Starlink at the time. Iridium were the kings of the Belief Glut, and their tragedy is a masterclass in the destructive power of cognitive bias.

Let's investigate their downfall through the lens of a broken BOODA loop:

- **B (Believe):** Their Core Belief, held with religious fervor, was that a huge market of global executives desperately needed to make calls from anywhere, at any time, and would pay any price for it. This was a fixed mindset, a non-negotiable dogma. Theirs was a "Me Against the World" posture, but the world they were fighting was the very market they claimed to serve. Their belief had mutated from a guiding vision into a defensive wall. **When Belief is used to block out the world rather than engage it, the 'B' in BOODA becomes a blindfold.**

- **O (Observe):** Here, the confirmation bias ran wild. While Iridium was launching satellites, the cellular phone was steadily taking over the planet. The Inner Gorilla doesn't just ignore data; it attacks it. When the cellular revolution appeared on their radar, Iridium's leadership didn't see a market shift; they saw an insult to their $5 billion ego. They were building a Rolls-Royce when Toyotas were flying off the assembly line. They held focus groups not to learn, but to validate. They listened only for the echoes of their own assumptions.

- **O (Orient):** Dragged under by sunk costs of a $5 billion satellite investment, they oriented every decision around protecting those satellites, not solving the customer's problem. The satellites were in the sky; the train had left the station. The idea of pivoting was unthinkable. Their identity was tied to the hardware, the grand gesture. To admit a mistake would be to admit the entire religion was false.

- **D (Decide) & A (Act):** They decided to act by launching their product in 1998: a clunky, brick-sized phone that cost $3,000 and charged $5 per minute for a call. They acted decisively, but in service of a reality that no longer existed, a reality their own biases had constructed.

The world's response was brutal and swift. Their target customers were perfectly happy with their new Nokia cell phones. Iridium, the company that promised to connect the world, couldn't get anyone to answer their call. In big cities they couldn't get a signal in the shadow of skyscrapers. They finally filed for bankruptcy in 1999. Iridium wasn't defeated by a competitor; they were defeated by their own flawed belief system. Their loop was a closed echo chamber, unable to process the overwhelming feedback the world was giving them. It was a Belief Glut, but one that could have been avoided if they knew how to Observe and Orient without the biases, with an open mind.

Iridium's story shows how a broken belief system leads to ruin. But what makes a healthy belief system so powerful? Why does the clarity of a founder have the power to mobilize an organization to do impossible things? The answer lies in the wiring of our brains.

Belief is a signal. And the human brain is exquisitely designed to tune into the signals of other brains, especially those of leaders. At MedXit the three founders feel like they belong together, they are sending out and receiving the same signal of their creed to make lives better through their medical data and system. They are open to push back on their own ideas, and hold conviction in their creed, not the specific execution of that vision.

When you observe someone acting with conviction, your brain activates cells called mirror neurons. These neurons fire as if you were performing the action yourself. You don't just see the conviction; you *feel* it. This is why a leader's authentic belief is contagious in a way corporate platitudes are not. Your team's brains can literally feel the difference between real conviction and empty talk. I think of it as the Tony Robbins effect—his energy and belief ripple through his audiences like a shock wave of faith—crushing doubt and negativity. The same thing is true with passionate founders. That conviction not only creates an unstoppable team, but it leads to a feeling of belonging which causes your brain to create chemicals like dopamine and norepinephrine that make you feel joy. Happiness at hyper-growth start ups doesn't come from fancy espresso machines. It comes from passion and conviction. It's your Belief, that creates these mirror neurons.

This neurological phenomenon goes even deeper than the happiness. When a team is truly aligned, their brainwaves can actually synchronize in a process called neural coupling. It's the neurological signature of a team that is "on the same wavelength.[1]" They are processing the world through a shared mental model,

---

1	Stephens, G. J., Silbert, L. J., & Hasson, U. (2010). *Speaker–listener neural coupling underlies successful communication.* PNAS (Proceedings of the National Academy of Sciences), 107(32), 14425-14430.

allowing them to react with seamless coordination—like a veteran pit crew or a squadron of fighter pilots. I saw this firsthand when I asked Gio and Sandra a specific question about a hospital in Belmont they were integrating and they both answered, in unison, the same exact words. All three of us laughed at that display of twin-like alignment.

Another thing to think about before we get to part two is the Belief Infection Rate. A founder is the primary carrier of the company's creed—patient zero. Your personal state—your inner game—determines the nature of the signal you transmit. A founder with a clear creed who has mastered their inner gorilla is like a super-spreader of Belief. Their Infection Rate is high and the "virus" they spread is one of focus, alignment, and trust. There is the anti-founder too. Someone who is still fighting the gorilla, seeing the world as a hostile place, will become a carrier of doubt and paranoia. Their inconsistency and defensiveness create cognitive dissonance, and the signal gets lost in static. This is how the sense of belonging deteriorates and eventually crushes the company. I've seen this most often with founders who start a company to make money, not because they had a pain they needed solved, or a passion for making something better.

The tools in Part 1—the BOODA Doctrine (Shared Belief Map, the Decision-Making Principles and the Creed)—are your way of ensuring that the belief you're spreading is pure, powerful, and capable of synchronizing your team into an unstoppable force.

You now stand on the bridge between idea and action, maybe it's more like a bridge you've built between two of those obstacles. You've used them to find your way, but there's more work to do. You have forged your creed, creating the clear, powerful signal your team can tune into. You have walked through the zoo and learned to recognize the beasts that can sabotage your journey. You have witnessed the ghost of Iridium, a stark reminder of what happens when belief becomes a fixed dogma. And you understand the deep neuroscience of why your conviction—and your mastery of your own inner state—is the most powerful tool you have. You have mapped the terrain inside your mind and the minds of your team.

Now, it is time to learn how to move along that map. It is time to step into the cockpit and master the disciplined, high-velocity loop of **Believe, Observe, Orient, Decide, and Act**. It is time to turn your belief into not just movement, but a movement.

PART II

THE LOOP OF CONQUEST (B.O.O.D.A.)

7

Observe – with an Unblinking Eye

I.

Thomas Lawaetz was dreaming of hockey.

Not the clean, elegant game where professionals race over pristine ice, but a frantic, nightmarish version on a vast, ink-black pond under a bruised-purple sky. He was the only player on the ice, skating on blades that felt dull, heavy, and perpetually stuck in patches of slush. Darkness was creeping up on him. There wasn't one puck; there were dozens. And each one was on fire. The smell of burning rubber stung his nose. Pucks smoldered on the cracked ice, spitting embers that hissed and popped. His job was to get to every single burning puck into the net where they flamed out before they melted through to the frigid, black water below.

He'd race to a burning puck in center ice, the cold air tearing at his lungs, his legs screaming in protest. Just as he flipped it toward the net to extinguish the flames with a spray of ice, he'd see the relentless glow of another one along the edge, flaring up. Then two more behind the other net. He wasn't playing a game; he was a one-man fire brigade on a rink that seemed like it was the size of Europe, and he was losing. The pucks were moving. The ice was thinning. It wasn't going to hold.

He woke up with a jolt, heart hammering against his ribs, not to an alarm, but to the familiar, insistent buzz of his phone on the nightstand. 1:17 a.m. The screen glowed with the ghosts of his dream. A dozen Slack notifications, a fresh volley of emails with subject lines flagged in angry bold font. The nightmare was just a high-speed, metaphorical replay of his reality.

Anja, his brilliant Operations Manager, needed his thoughts on their first possible German clinic, but Thomas wanted to see a deeper competitor analysis before he moved forward. Lars in Denmark was reporting that their primary syringe supplier had just missed a critical delivery, threatening their Q4 patient target. Sanne in Sweden had a software glitch that was backing up patient intake, and the dev team was arguing about the fix. As he shook the hockey nightmare out of his head, he thought maybe the pucks were real, after all, and they were all on fire.

This was Thomas's life as the founder of the rapidly scaling Nordic Health Group. From the outside, it was a spectacular success: 54 specialized vein clinics across five countries, with a bold vision for 400 in the next five years. On the inside, it was a firefighter's dream every single day. A new challenge, a deep urgency, clear success and failure. He was brilliant, driven, and completely, utterly exhausted from chasing the pucks. The biggest burning puck of them all was this German opportunity Anja was spearheading. The opportunity was massive, but with an unknown cost. In Germany, to run specialized vein clinics around the country, regulations required owning a traditional hospital to support those clinics. This law created a complicated and very costly prerequisite, but that didn't stop Thomas. He spent months searching and eventually found a private hospital for sale. The problem was it was losing a couple million euro a year, and to make acquiring it even more intimidating - he had no idea how to run a hospital. His private equity partners had the capital already lined up to buy the hospital and to put up several clinics. He negotiated a sale-leaseback with a real estate financier to free up more cash. The deal was on the table. All he had to do was sign.

The entire future of the company's expansion seemed to hinge on this single, smoldering decision. He kept looking for more data, and then pushed Anja to do more research, then he spun back to talk to more finance guys. He was skating on a single blade, leaning over, going in circles. How does a founder escape this spiral? The answer, improbably, lies not in a business school textbook, but on the frozen ponds of Brantford, Ontario. The legendary Wayne Gretzky, the most dominant player in the history of the sport, famously explained his genius this way: "I skate to where the puck is going to be, not where it has been."

The quote is so famous it's become a cliché. But it's often misunderstood. Gretzky wasn't a psychic, he was a student. As a young boy, he'd sit in front of a grainy black-and-white television, take out a fresh sheet of white paper and a pencil, then from the moment the puck dropped he would trace its path on a diagram of a rink, over and over, until the patterns were etched into his subconscious. He wasn't watching the puck; he was learning the system, the geometry of the game. He was a master observer who had built such a powerful predictive model in his head that he could process all the variables—the speed of the players, the angles of their skates, the physics of a bouncing puck—and see the future state of the system faster than anyone else. His ability to predict the outcome is just what the brain is designed to do, so he was always less surprised than other players and more accurate in his predictions. He did the hard work of learning the system, its inputs and pressure points. The Nordic Health team often felt like they were watching things unfold for the first time, they seemed to be skating toward where the puck is, and by the time they got there it was gone.

There was no doubt that Thomas had a world-changing Belief, his team was plowing their way across the Gap—knocking down obstacles like weak defensemen. They had a Shared Belief Map and knew where they wanted to go with their goal of 400 clinics across Europe. What he lacked was a doctrine to observe the external forces like the market. He was about to learn that you can't skate to where the puck is going to be if you're constantly bumping into your teammates. This chapter is about how to see the ice. It's about a radical doctrine for you, born in the cockpit of a fighter jet, that provides a blueprint for how to process reality and make decisions at a speed that seems like magic. It starts with a man who was arguably the greatest fighter pilot who ever lived, yet a man who never shot down an enemy plane.

II.

John Boyd was a character straight out of a Michael Lewis book: a hulking, cigar-chomping, intellectually ferocious Air Force colonel who was a walking middle finger to the defense-industrial establishment. He was the best fighter pilot instructor in the USA, so ostensibly the best in the world, but he only saw short period of active duty in Korea and was never in a real life-or-death dogfight himself. But as an instructor he had no equal. He was so good he was known as "40-Second Boyd" because he had a standing bet with any pilot coming in for air-to-air combat training. Boyd would wager a steak dinner that he could defeat the student in a dogfight in under 40 seconds. The unbelievable kicker? Boyd let the challenger start directly behind him, on his six, in a position of perfect advantage. Imagine being in that student's cockpit. You're locked on Boyd's tail, you've done this countless times back at your squadron, but this is the first time at the elite training school. The sky is yours. All you have to do is a quick missile-lock and then squeeze the trigger. But before you can, Boyd's jet does something impossible. His plane brakes, it jukes, it turns over and dives at the same time. Boyd seems to defy the laws of motion, and you push your stick down trying desperately to keep up with each move, but you're now three moves behind and you're only 12 seconds into the fight. The world outside your canopy becomes a blur of blue and brown. Your stomach lurches as you squeeze your abs and t'aint to fight the G forces, your noggin bouncing like a bobble-head doll. By the time your brain catches up, Boyd is no longer your target. He's on *your* six, and the only thing you see is the nose of his plane, calm and steady, ready for the kill shot. He never lost.

Boyd wasn't just a gifted pilot; he was a physicist of aerial combat, obsessed with understanding the "why" behind his own talent. That obsession led him to develop the OODA loop you learned about in Part 1. Boyd's central insight was that all conflict is a duel between decision cycles. The one who can execute the loop faster and more effectively will win, every time. By getting "inside" your opponent's decision cycle, you force them to react to a world that you have already changed.

You force your opponent to be reactive, confused, and ultimately, irrelevant. If you're an 70's or 80's kid you watched a technology dogfight play out in slow motion, not with jets, but with calls, mini keyboards, and eventually selfies.

In 2006, the undisputed champion of the sky—the "40-Second Boyd" of the corporate communication world—was BlackBerry. I carried mine around like a fashion accessory. Blackberry owned the pocket of every CEO, politician, banker, and self-important executive on the planet, including the President of the United States. Their advantage seemed unassailable, their patented mini-keyboard was so comfortable and easy to use; how could they lose. But what happens when you are the market leader and you slow your BOODA loop? You start to get stuck after the Believe stage. You also *assume* you've got the B—"Our Core Beliefs haven't changed in 10 years and our hypotheses don't need to be proven—we're the best!" When you skip analyzing the B and your SBM, that means you're in an OODA loop of frozen data.

BlackBerry's OODA loop had become glacial, and it was arrogant, take a look:

- **Observe:** *Our users are addicted. They call it a 'CrackBerry.' Look at all those 'Sent from my BlackBerry' email signatures. The market is strong and we own it.*
- **Orient:** *The smartphone is an email device. It's for serious business. People need physical keyboards to type efficiently. That's our moat. This 'touch-screen' stuff is a toy. And a camera? Get real.*
- **Decide:** *Let's form a committee to make our trackball slightly better and launch the 'Pearl' to appeal to the consumer market. But don't mess with the keyboard.*
- **Act:** *Ship another million units of the Curve. Ignore the CEO's belief that the Internet was where the puck was going. Lack of a SBM allowed the illusion of agreement to kill the company.*

Meanwhile, in Cupertino, California Steve Jobs saw an opportunity and he had Apple running a different BOODA loop entirely.

- **Believe:** *The future of computing will be in your pocket. The interface and experience must be easy and elegant, and people will fall in love with it. This is a movement that goes way beyond email.*
- **Observe:** *Everyone just accepts their phone. They are ugly, clunky, and complicated to change and set-up. The real opportunity isn't a better email machine; it's a pocket-sized computer. Even with music, maps, and pictures. Fun, useful stuff. The mobile internet is the puck, and it's heading for a totally different part of the ice.*
- **Orient:** *To win, the entire front of the device must be a screen. The 'app' will be the new unit of value, not the keyboard. We have to build a whole new operating system that makes the internet, not email, the main event. We need to encourage people to build apps.*
- **Decide:** *Bet the entire company on a single, unproven, keyboard-less device. We will call it the iPhone.*
- **Act:** *Ship it.*

By the time BlackBerry's leadership finally *Observed* that the world had changed, *Oriented* themselves to the new reality of software, apps and touch-screens, and *Decided* to launch their own sad, desperate imitation (remember the BlackBerry Storm, anyone?), Apple was already skating to the next spot on the ice: the App Store and the iPhone 3G with pictures and music.

Apple got "inside" BlackBerry's decision cycle. They forced an entire industry to react to a world that no longer existed. The BOODA Doctrine is so effective because if you follow it, you realize that you don't need competitors to incite you to do faster, more effective loops. You can do it yourself, if of course you are curious enough to make sure you are not stuck in a Belief Glut.

In 2007, Justin Kan was the most "watched" man on Earth, but he was also the mayor of a village called the Belief Glut. He spent every waking second wearing a head-mounted camera, streaming his life 24/7 to the world over the Internet. Technically, it was nearly a miracle—a feat of engineering that solved the "how" of live streaming years before the rest of the world.

Justin and his team had a full tank of Internal Belief. They were "high on their own supply," like we were at DaVinci 3.0. They were convinced that "lifecasting" was the future of entertainment and their technical genius was proof. But while their internal score was a 10, their External Belief looked like a ghost town. People tuned in for the novelty, but the data was screaming a truth they didn't want to hear; watching a guy eat cereal or sleep isn't a business; it's a vanity project.

Justin.tv as a company was living in the Belief Glut—where a founder's ego refuses to see reality. It's where you mortgage the house, burn your family's support, and sprint toward a cliff because you've confused being a "Visionary" with being "Right."

Stubbornness can put blinders on your mind. It tells you that if the market isn't buying, they just "don't get it" yet. But the BOODA Doctrine isn't a suicide pact; it's an agile navigation system that forces you to see reality.

Justin.tv survived because they chose to Observe with surgical precision. They saw a small, weird cluster of users on their platform who weren't streaming their lives—they were streaming their video game matches.

Instead of staying stubborn and forcing the "lifecasting" vision, the team Re-Oriented. They tore down their old model and created a new Hypothesis: Users won't pay to see someone's life but they will pay $XX a month to see world-class gamers in action. Now it was up to them to prove this Hypothesis right, while killing the old Hypothesis that people would pay to livestream their life.

They pivoted. They scrapped the "Justin" in Justin.tv and built Twitch. They didn't "Believe harder" in a failing vision; they used the BOODA loop to step off the island of delusion and onto the bridge of market-validated data. Then they became a Unicorn.

The lesson for every Maverick is this: If you find yourself preaching to an empty cathedral where the only one clapping is you, you aren't crossing a Gap. You are stuck in a Glut. And in the world of startups, the only thing more expensive than building a company is building a hallucination.

III.

Cadence replaces chaos with the BOODA Doctrine. The Nordic Health Group knew the lesson, but they didn't yet know the why.

To understand why a brilliant founder like Thomas at Nordic Health could become his own bottleneck, you have to step back inside the Miller Lab at MIT, that you first saw in Chapter 3. Picture it: the quiet hum of servers, whiteboards covered in a cryptic calculus of brainwave frequencies and synaptic models, and at the center, Dr. Earl Miller, moving with the unhurried calm of someone who intimately understands the noisy chaos of the human mind and the penalties of multi-switching.

You already know that Miller's research shows multitasking is just a myth. He also goes further and describes our attention in two very specific ways it's either a "floodlight" or a "spotlight." The floodlight is our wide-angle, ambient attention, constantly scanning for threats and opportunities, always looking at the big picture, always trying to predict what's next. Like Gretzky seeing the whole rink. The spotlight is our focused, narrow-beam attention that we direct at a single task. The human brain, he has proven, cannot run two spotlights at the same time. The spotlight is used for situations like walking into a crowded café and looking for the friend you are supposed to meet there—your gaze jumps face to face putting your spotlight on one person's features, looking for your pal. What we call multitasking (trying to look for your friend and order a cappuccino at the same time) is task-switching—rapidly toggling our single spotlight back and forth. Remember that every switch comes with a heavy cognitive cost, a tax on your time and mental energy. It's a neurological thief that steals your focus and drains your willpower. What Thomas needed was more time to use his floodlight to get from 54 to 400 clinics. He knew of a pretty successful founder who had done just that during the height of the dot.com days.

Amazon's genius for organizational design stands out because they were masters at using the spotlight in the right moment. Jeff Bezos recognized that in a company as vast as Amazon, making progress on new, important ideas was nearly impossible if they were just one of ten priorities on a manager's plate—that's the floodlight. The "spotlight" of the organization was too diffuse, flickering across too many targets. So he invented the concept of a Single-Threaded Owner (STO) putting a spotlight on just one rock.

An STO's world shrinks to a single outcome. One of Amazon's most impactful employees, Andy Jassy, wasn't "also" responsible for cloud computing during a new project called Amazon Web Services (AWS); it was his single thread. He owned it. Dave Limp wasn't just managing a portfolio of hardware projects; Kindle was his single obsession. An STO isn't a title; it's a way of focusing the company's limited and precious attention to accelerate a specific BOODA loop. It's a declaration that one thing matters so much, we are dedicating one of our best minds to it, and nothing else; you run a spotlight on this loop and you work through it ferociously. Within Amazon the STO strategy effectively created founders just like you and me, but within the confines of the world's biggest company.

Thomas, in his heroic effort to be everywhere, had made himself the *Anti-Single-Threaded Owner* of *everything*. While he was on a Zoom call about the German launch, he was simultaneously Slacking the Danish team about their supplier issue. He thought he was being efficient. In reality, he was paying a massive cognitive tax. While Anja was talking about the German market details, he switched back to the Slack conversation, and continued to give Anja a distracted "uh-huh," every now and then. When he did focus on her, he had to go back to where he left off, mentally rewind to get the context and then listen (remember multi-tasking doesn't exist). This switching left a lot of blank spots because Thomas was not truly present. He missed a key detail in Anja's presentation, forcing a follow-up meeting, which delayed the possible deal signing by another week, this mistake, in turn, pushed back the hiring of another clinic's lead physician. His multitasking wasn't just a personal habit; it was a systemic brake on the entire company.

IV.

There is no business school case study that can prepare you for the exquisite torture of being right too early. It's a lesson that is seared into my memory, a lesson I learned in the most painful way possible with my company ServerVault. We had basically invented the cloud in 1999, four years before AWS was a glimmer in Bezos's eye (or more accurately a glimmer in Andy Jassy's eye, the STO at Amazon Web Services). I accurately saw where the puck was going; computing power as a utility, not a hardware product. And then we fell flat on our faces.

Why? To understand, you have to travel with me to a Hogwarts-like hall at University College London and try to keep up with the mind of our friend Dr. Karl Friston. Friston's Free Energy Principle you read about earlier is one of the most ambitious ideas in modern neuroscience. It argues that the brain is not a passive camera taking in reality; it's a prediction engine. What you perceive as "reality" is a controlled hallucination, a story your brain tells itself based on past experiences, a story which is constantly being updated by sensory input.

The only time you truly "observe" something is when incoming data contradicts your brain's prediction. This creates what Friston calls "free energy" or surprise—a prediction error. Think of your brain as a thermostat set to 70 degrees. It predicts the room will be 70 degrees. If someone opens a window in winter and the temperature plummets, the thermostat doesn't just passively record the new temperature. It screams, "Prediction error!" and kicks on the furnace to close the gap between prediction and reality. The entire purpose of your brain is to minimize that kind of surprise.

At ServerVault, the market met our vision with massive prediction error— what the hell are you offering? We were selling "virtual private data centers" to people whose predictive model was based on the physical server (or mainframe) in a locked room down the hall from their office. Our prospects' brains generated a mountain of free energy when we talked to them about our offerings. They believed data had to sit in their offices, on their computers; like contracts had to be in their file cabinets at the same headquarters. The prediction error was too great for them to get their minds around. I'll never forget meeting with the CIO from a Fortune 500 company, who leaned across the table and said, "Son, the day I let my company's data leave this building is the day I hand in my resignation." He wasn't being difficult; his brain was simply rejecting a reality that was too surprising to process. The puck was coming to us, but not very quickly it seemed.

I felt like I was slap, slap, slapping my stick on the ice to let my teammates know I was open and no one could hear me.

If you metaphorically watched the puck's trajectory across the ice it was coming in our general direction, but it stopped along the way in what were called colocation centers. Instead of creating a complete cloud, like we did at ServerVault, colocation facilities only sold the fenced-in cages inside a big warehouse, like boarding kennels for servers. The companies who moved their internal data center to colocation centers needed to bring their own engineers in to set up and run their own servers. That was the first place the puck stopped—meanwhile I was still waiting in the slot for a one-timer, and I'd wait until my shoulders got too tired to hold up the stick. We were too early. I knew the puck would get to us eventually. Thankfully we had an incredible team that kept Believing.

That initial failure—the searing, humiliating gap between our vision and the world's belief—ignited my twenty-year obsession that led to this book.

At Nordic Health Group, Thomas's hesitation, his constant requests for "more data," was his brain's attempt to minimize uncertainty. He was afraid of the prediction error that would come from the Germany launch. His amygdala, the brain's ancient warning system, was treating the uncertainty like a lion in the grass. For him to feel safer he needed the BOODA Doctrine which laid out his SBM and Decision Making Principles, they are like a Zulu warrior's shield for uncertainty. BOODA Doctrine turns a potentially catastrophic prediction error into a manageable, data-generating experiment. It gives a founder the courage to go full throttle, knowing they have enough fuel to handle all the twists and turns.

V.

A few weeks after his dream, Thomas and I talked about the emerging challenge of scaling things up. We walked through his existing operating strategy with the BOODA loop and expanded it to codify roles, ownership and decision cadence. He convened his executive team on Zoom. He didn't open with an agenda or a slide deck. He told them about his hockey-player/firefighter's dream. He told them about Wayne Gretzky.

"I've been chasing pucks," he said, the vulnerability in his voice capturing their full attention. "All of them, all day. Like playing hockey, it's fun, but it's slowing us down. My job isn't to be the best player. My job is to be the coach. From now on, our company's job is not to chase the puck. Our job is to see the ice."

A great NHL coach isn't watching the puck, he's watching the geometry. He sees the defenseman's hand slide down the stick a fraction of a second too early, opening up a passing lane. He'll see the forward gliding into a soft spot in the defensive zone away from the boards, an area of open ice that will become dangerous in three heartbeats. One, two, three—there goes the pass. You'll hear the coach yell "Get pucks deep!" when he notices his offensive players are getting stopped in the neutral zone at the middle of the rink. He's not chasing a puck. He will change tactics when he sees the subtle fatigue in his team's center, the way he's a half-step slower getting up the ice, so rather than skate with the puck toward the net, he changes strategy to pass the puck deep to the other end of the ice, then players follow in after it. Great coaches are not watching the game as it is; they are watching the game as it is *about to be*. What are you watching as a founder? Thomas was watching chaos, putting a spotlight on small challenges across the 54 locations and he now had a fix. Now he could start using his floodlight to cast a glow on the big picture.

Thomas laid out a clear operating structure for his team, consistent with the BOODA Doctrine. The country managers were no longer just heads of their regions; they were the Single-Threaded Owners of their markets, they were to think like founders. Their job was to run their own, independent BOODA loops, come up with their own SBM, test their Hypothesis and run loops. The dashboards that once fed only Thomas's screen were made public for all the employees to see. The goal wasn't to report up to a bottleneck; it was to learn and act, fast, and to share those learnings across the system.

The shift was palpable, the leadership team could feel it even through the Zoom screen. Anja's expression, a mask of patient frustration for weeks, softened into a look of fierce determination. The Slack channel, usually a stream of questions directed at Thomas, lit up with his leaders talking to each other.

Even if you aren't a fan of the NHL you still have probably heard of Wayne Gretzky; but you likely haven't heard of Conner McDavid. He's the fastest skater in the NHL. He won the All-Star fastest player competition a record four times. He's amassed over 1,100 points in his career. But it's not just his speed that sets him apart. McDavid is challenged every year for his title of fastest skater and there are plenty of close challenges and sometimes other skaters are faster than him. But when it comes to actual game performance none of those speed challengers are even close to McDavid. None of them have his point totals, or his ability to make things happen especially during the play-offs. He can skate like rocket ship exploding from a dead stop, *and* he can control that slippery little piece of rubber at the same time. In the world of sports, McDavid is a Unicorn.

And what is true for a player like Gretzky or McDavid or any NHL all-star coach on the bench is true for a founder in a market. The world of startups is a chaotic rink of its own, filled with customer requests, competitor moves, technological shifts, and market noise. The founder who wins is the one who can see the ice, the one who knows a McDavid or Gretzky when they walk through the door and is so passionate in his Belief that it's contagious to an all-star who is dedicated to winning. A great founder like you has to recognize the player who can both skate fast and stick handle at top speed. The ones who don't chase the pucks, they see the underlying patterns, the opening lanes, the coming opportunities. They are the ones who skate to where their market is going to be, arriving just as the puck does, while their competitors are still chasing it into the corner. They are the ones who know the pain they solve. Thomas was now enabling his country managers to become all-stars. He was teaching them to skate fast and stick handle at the same time.

I see hundreds of deals a year for the venture firms I work with and for my own investing. Assessing the founders is the most critical step: are they passionate about dominating their market, are they solving their own pain and do they understand the ecosystem enough to skate to where the puck will be (but not too early). Finally, is this a must-have or nice to have (Painkillers vs Vitamins). I saw a fantastic idea this year for a feminine products company that was basically a Dollar Shave Club for tampons. Women could either subscribe for a monthly fee and ship to their home or the company would set up a program at their work place (as an employee benefit). There was no competition in the space, and it seemed like a great idea. The problem was it was started by two guys out of business school looking for a company to build and sell. Remember when I mentioned passion and scratching your own itch? They had no experience in the women's health market, they didn't know first-hand the pain they needed to solve—it was just a good idea. Since there were no women on the founding team, I passed. I want to work with founders who know the pain and can see around players to where the puck will be. Part of seeing where the puck will be is also recognizing technical breakthroughs that can be used in different ways than may have originally been imagined.

Did you think of generative artificial intelligence in 2015? Maybe you toyed with some machine learning protocols if you were forward thinking but certainly not like we know AI today. However, in 2015 Sam Altman started Open AI with the vision of where AI would go. It wasn't until the end of November 2022 that ChatGPT was released, and Altman was alone in front of the net with the puck tapping in an easy goal. Everyone else had to play catch-up. Thomas, at Nordic Health, comes from a family of surgeons and health-care experts. He knows the space. His family sat around the dinner table at Christmas talking about *surgery and shifts*. He is the right guy to dominate this market.

A month after our first meeting, I sat in on another executive call with the Nordic Health team. It was half as long and ten times as productive. I was seeing the magic of the BOODA loop working firsthand. Sanne wasn't asking for permission; she was reporting on the patient acquisition data from the first two weeks of the Gothenburg launch. Lars in Denmark shared a "Golden Poop" story about a supplier mistake that led them to discover a more reliable, lower-cost alternative, an insight the UK team was now acting on.

Thomas barely spoke. He listened. He asked questions. He was observing the geometry with the power of a single floodlight. He had stopped being the frantic, exhausted player and had become the architect of a team that could see the ice. He closed his laptop at the end of the day, not with the familiar bone-deep weariness, but with a sense of calm control he hadn't felt in years. There were still fires, there always would be, and in fact he still liked the challenge of putting out those little flare ups, they made him feel productive and challenged. But now, he had a whole team of firefighters on a regular schedule with a rhythm and format for weekly BOODA Stand-Up meetings. They had their Doctrine for hyper-growth.

This ability to "see the ice" is what separates the good from the great. It's a kind of operational clairvoyance. The great coach or player isn't just faster on their skates or better at understanding defenses. They are faster at *thinking*. They process information, build a model of reality, and act on it more quickly and efficiently than anyone else in the arena (this is the essence of BOODA). If you want to build a unicorn, and scale at hyper-growth you need to operate in a different temporal dimension.

These are the realities around the physics of Observation, the first O. A founder who is constantly "multitasking"—checking email while on a Zoom call, calculating payroll while listening to a product pitch—is not observing 100%

of anything. She is just paying a massive cognitive tax, her single spotlight flickering uselessly across a dozen different targets. **She lacks one thing that great founders can call up at will—presence.**

A Shared Belief Map helps us focus our limited attention. When you did your SBM exercise, how many items ended up in your Garage? Probably 5-10. You chose 6-8 things that made it to your SBM, but left those Garage items for later evolution. Imagine if your company didn't implement the BOODA Doctrine—you'd have 20 or 25 things to "focus" on. I've seen this countless times in post-Series A companies who now have resources (lots of cash) and decide to branch out to new products, new markets, new marketing. They don't realize that every new area they branch into is like starting another company from scratch. And often when they get these expansion ideas they are not coming from a customer, but rather a developer or product manager. Their Belief Gap was closing but now adding other products or services or markets means you are widening that Gap, and potentially creating doubt in your own teammates and internal believers as well as the outside.

This brings us to the critical connection between Belief, doubt, fear, and observation. When your internal model of the world is weak, inaccurate, or in conflict with itself, your brain is constantly being surprised. It's generating a massive amount of free energy. It is, in a very real sense, in a state of chronic fear or anxiety. This reaction is similar with doubt just not as strong as fear.

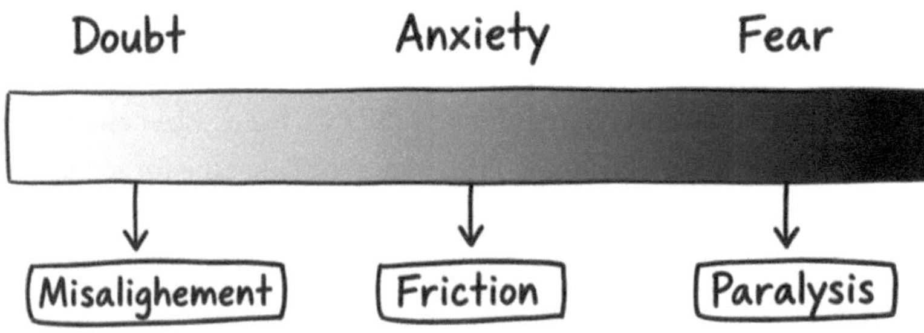

Figure 16—the slower you are to stop the source of anxiety the more likely it is to escalate toward fear

Doubt is not triggered by your amygdala like fear, but more your Anterior Cingulate Cortex (ACC), which is often referenced as your courage center. It's like your brain's speed bump trying to get you to slow down when something doesn't seem quite right. The question you need to ask is: seem right compared to what?

What we do is compare the present to all the information that was programmed into our subconscious brain in the past, most of our subconscious data comes from when we were a child. Your subconscious is your point of reference, so anything that doesn't fit into your model, even a little bit, will bring up the feeling of doubt or even fear. When it comes to hyper-scaling a business, doubt is deadly.

Doubt is the neurological cost of a misaligned team. I didn't see this clearly until I started working with venture-backed companies as a board member and advisor. It literally took me 20 years to see the patterns and look at the journey from an observer's perspective and not a participant's perspective. I'm sure there are smarter people who saw the pattern much quicker, but the key to falling victim to doubt is that you develop a growth mindset and start looking for patterns. I had an awareness of the patterns of Belief and Doubt at my companies (particularly after ServerVault) but I needed more clarity. Like Gretzky, when you see enough hockey games you can recognize those patterns and that's what led me to the clarity of The Founder's Creed. If your team has a group of big brains that are constantly surprising each other because they are not aligned with the SBM that's when you start losing key employees, dropping the ball on customers and missing key objectives. It's Creed drift - but it's not amygdala driven fear (which can lead to operational paralysis) if it gets worse your team goes from doubt to anxiety and that's friction, it kills momentum. Your collective brain is a storm of free energy. You've got a company in a state of perpetual, low-grade fear. Most times the founder cannot see the ice clearly because your teammates are all hallucinating a different game. There is one founder who let his team know clearly where their key insights should come into play during the observation phase and that's simply by asking customers the right questions.

Nexthink is one of Switzerland's newest unicorns—they sold a majority stake to a private equity firm in 2025 at a valuation of three billion dollars. One of the founders, Patrick Hertzog and his team weren't just building a product; they were trying to find a name for a problem no one else had fully defined. They found this problem by running so many BOODA loops it became obvious. When I went to the top of Lake Geneva in the idyllic city of Lausanne, I met Patrick at EPFL University, the MIT of Switzerland. He said the first few years of the business they were fixing small problems and trying to figure out where the big opportunity was. He felt in his bones there was something bigger than IT set up or desktop support. They believed they could make great products, but they were solving small problems. After a new release or client on-boarding, in the Observation phase, they would ask their clients and prospects where the pain was. People kept saying the intrusion detection system works but it's a nightmare to use, the CRM is already integrated but it takes hours to do routine stuff. They saw employees wasting hours every week on calls with tech support. They finally came to Believe companies would be better off if their employees had a better digital experience in all facets of their job. This Observation led to them Orienting around how to create a solution—then Deciding which direction to go and delivering. Then they did it again, and again, and again. The analysts—Gartner, Forrester, the usual suspects—were content to put them in familiar boxes: data center provisioning, maybe desktop management. But Patrick knew that wasn't right. He was observing something different; he was seeing from the eyes of hundreds of customers. Analysts see from their own eyes. Nexthink saw a huge pain point that was unserved. Employees were struggling with their digital experience, and no one had created a solution that could solve it. Patrick lived by one rule that he shared with all the employees—sell pain killers not vitamins . He had finally discovered a massive pain.

Nexthink did what great Observers do: they asked better questions. They talked to customers not just about what tools they used, but about what hurt. When they asked enough questions, they got to the root of the problem and solved it. They knew they weren't selling a vitamin, they were doing just what Patrick had led them to do, selling a painkiller. That painkiller was something they created a name for - DEX—Digital Employee Experience.

It took a couple of years, but eventually the market caught up. Gartner soon created a category for DEX, and suddenly Nexthink wasn't just a company; it was a category leader in the upper right-hand corner of that Magic Quadrant. Like many of the companies you've learned about in Founder's Creed, they didn't build a product or service, they started a movement. They believed an employee's experience at work with the technology they interacted with all day long was a category all of its own. That's the power of observing the right things and not letting old labels define your new reality, or blind your observation. So ask yourself—are you selling a painkiller or a vitamin?

Back in Denmark at Nordic Health, Thomas implemented a critical principle to hyper-growth once he realized it's not just about having a visionary leader who sees the future. It's about building a team with a shared model of reality so powerful that they can all see the same future together, and they each act in the best interest of those goals. Team alignment closes the internal Belief Gap, and turns big obstacles into the way forward because the team is surmounting them together. The collective goal in the Observe cycle is that the entire team is seeing everything that reveals itself—but it's not enough to see the entire ice. You have to use experience, education, upbringing, all to put yourself in the right frame of mind to actual decide and act, and that's where Thomas was stuck right now. He believes 400 clinics are coming in the next five years but right now he can't get past this latest one.

What's coming in the next five years for you and what's keeping you from compressing your BOODA loops today?

8

The Expert's Blindfold

I.

The most dangerous thing a founder can do is assume they see the world as it is. To coin an old phrase; if you assume it doesn't just make an ass out of you and me, it can be deadly.

In aviation, there's a plane with a reputation so specific it earned a nickname that pilots still whisper with a mix of respect and dread: the V-Tail Doctor Killer. The aircraft is an old version of the Beechcraft Bonanza, a sleek, high-performance single-engine plane that looks like success. It's fast, beautifully engineered, and forgiving—right up until it isn't. Early versions were built with a distinctive V-shaped tail, an elegant design that reduced drag and increased speed. On paper, it was a masterpiece. In practice, it became a death trap for a very specific kind of pilot. Doctors.

The nickname didn't emerge because doctors are reckless. Quite the opposite. They're highly intelligent experts who spend their professional lives making life-or-death decisions under pressure. They trust their judgment because, most of the time, that judgment is right. And that's exactly the problem.

A V-Tail Bonanza doesn't kill bad pilots. It kills confident ones. Pilots who have logged enough hours to believe instinct can replace procedure. Pilots who read weather reports and see conditions they would have avoided when they first started flying and think, "I've got this." Pilots whose expertise convinces them they can bend reality just a little—and then a little more—until the wind-shear and mountain face arrives in front of them sooner than expected, or the V-tail gets ripped off in a thunder cloud. The plane isn't the killer. Orientation is.

Orientation has five categories that apply to business as well as aviation. I know this structure intimately, because DaVinci was my V-Tail Sweendawg killer. My "Prior Experience" (First element) was decades of building data centers, designing high-efficiency systems, and solving problems smarter people had ignored or failed at. I have 13 patents in my name, so I've got outside validation. I have loads of awards. My "Genetic Heritage" (Second Element) was Irish stubbornness fused with MIT-honed systems-thinking. My "Cultural Tradition" (Third Element) was being a repeat CEO who could will a company into existence through sheer conviction. My "New Information" (Fourth Element) was having the ear of the top Bitcoin Miner CEOs who were begging for a more efficient mining system. And finally, the Analysis & Synthesis (Fifth Element) told me that tearing down old mining equipment and stripping out inefficiency would create an elegant and efficient solution. Every piece of my past told me: You're right. Keep on going.

Our Orientation was entirely internal. We were so focused on our own elegant "surgery"—the immersion-cooling tech, the modular design—that we missed the most basic pre-op prep work. When we were in the Belief Glut, gasping for air, we went to our lead investor and asked them to become our first customer. Their emphatic no was the challenge we ignored, the storm cloud on our radar. We built a $2 million MVP when we should have built a $50,000 protype and let them see that first, then we would have discovered the issues that eventually killed us and still had $1.95 million in the bank.

But it wasn't an obstacle that was showing us the way, it certainly wasn't one we could metabolize. It was a fatal one. A prospect pointed out the simple, devastating flaw we had failed to Orient to: Antminer, the primary chip manufacturer, would void the warranty on their multi-thousand-dollar ASIC chips the moment they were submerged in our cooling fluid.

It was a classic "V-Tail" blind spot. We were the "Doctor Pilots," so convinced of our own genius that we never read the manufacturer's warning label. That single, missed observation, which our flawed Orientation had dismissed as "just a detail," was the final nail in our coffin. A co-pilot might have saved us—but I was a sole founder.

Think of it this way: The Doctor Pilot doesn't just ignore the storm clouds; his expert brain 'autocompletes' the image of a basically clear sky because that is what his successful past predicts. Remember the brain is a prediction engine, first and foremost. The diversity of predictions increases the number of options. You, as the founder and the master of your universe, can become a victim of your own efficiency. The very expertise that made you a successful founder is the same biological mechanism, if you aren't aware of it, that will prevent you from Orienting. Your expertise crops your ability to see new threats. That's the start of your eventual downfall. Your past wins have essentially 'pre-loaded' your perspective.

And that's why this chapter matters more than any other in the Doctrine. Because your biggest risk as a founder isn't making the wrong decision. It's believing the wrong thing is obviously right. The realization that the gap between what you think the world is and what it actually is—is the entire point of Orientation. Because if you get it wrong it eats away at the most precious resource you have. Not employees, not customers, not investors. Time.

At DaVinci we built an immersion-cooled bitcoin mining system around a component we didn't control — and a warranty condition that explicitly forbade the thing that made our design so effective. It wasn't an engineering flaw. It wasn't even arrogance. It was momentum with too much faith, and not enough attention to detail. I autocompleted the operational permissions. In all my prior companies we bought millions of dollars in hardware, the supplying company always helped us succeed with it. That has been my career experience—when I bought new servers, Sun, or Cisco or Akami would come into our data center and help us get the most from them. A supplier's job is to help us succeed not hold us back. It never occurred to me Antminer would hinder our progress.

That is Orientation failure in its purest form. It's where your past, your biases, your identity, your previous wins, and your cultural wiring collide with the data you've just Observed. Orientation is where founders distort reality without realizing they're doing it. It's where DaVinci died long before the market crashed.

High-performance tools, like maneuverability and speed, amplify whatever worldview you bring into the cockpit. In the hands of a disciplined novice, the

Bonanza is safe. In the hands of an overconfident expert, it became lethal. The danger isn't ignorance. The danger is autocomplete—the brain filling in reality with what it expects to see.

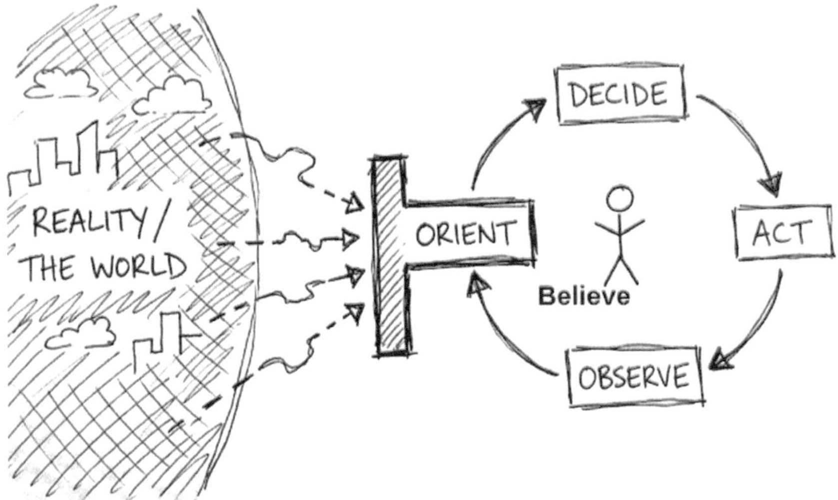

Figure 17—Orientation is our custom filter on reality.

We are all, to borrow a phrase from the military strategist John Boyd, prisoners of our own Orientation. And sometimes, the most profound realization about the world—the one that will ultimately forge your Unicorn—happens not in a boardroom, but in the most mundane of settings. For Thomas Lawaetz, the founder of Nordic Health Group, it happened at the family kitchen table when he was a teenager living life in the suburbs of Copenhagen, Denmark.

Thomas grew up in a house filled with the quiet, confident air of medical professionals. His parents, uncles, aunts, and grandparents were doctors and nurses. The dinner table conversation wasn't about politics or the local football team; it was about the Danish healthcare system. But as a teenager, Thomas started to notice a peculiar, curious pattern in the stories being told. A pattern that didn't make sense to his young, inquisitive mind.

"What I took away from those dinner conversations was how little they actually talked about the outcome of the surgery or the interests of the patients," Thomas recalled. "They were talking much more about getting this or that role, rising in the hierarchy, getting a promotion, working the political system, getting a grant or funded for this or that or downsizing or upsizing or resources being shifted around, but not about patients."

Think about that for a moment. You have a room full of brilliant, highly-trained, compassionate people—people who have sworn an oath to heal—and their professional lives are dominated not by the patient, the customer, but by the internal politics of the institution. The conversations were hardly ever about the success of a complex surgery; they were about the success of the surgeon's career.

The lack of patient talk was Thomas's eureka moment: the seemingly small, counterintuitive detail that unlocks a massive, hidden truth. It was a surprise, but great founders look for the surprises, look for prediction error. The truth he stumbled upon was that the entire system was suffering from a catastrophic failure of Orientation. The doctors were Orienting themselves not to the mission (patient care), but to the incentive structure (political advancement and resource control).

The incentive system had created a blind spot so large it swallowed the entire purpose of the organization. The surgeons, with their "God complex" saw themselves as the best at everything. They were operating in a monoculture of expertise, where their collective belief in their own infallibility meant they couldn't see the fundamental flaw in their worldview. They were Observing the hospital, but they were Orienting to the wrong battle.

Thomas's single Belief—the realization that the system's incentives had warped the professionals' worldview—evolved into the founding Creed of Nordic Health Group. Patient first and to the highest quality was the "B" that would precede Thomas's entire BOODA loop.

II.

People talk about the military OODA loop like it's a sequence—Observe, Orient, Decide, Act—but Boyd saw Orientation as the gravitational center, the force that bends everything around it and determines which observations matter and which should be ignored. The right level of curiosity at this phase can help you determine which decisions are obvious and which would never occur to you. Two people can look at the same data and walk away believing they've seen different worlds. And in a way, they have.

Orientation is shaped by five forces: prior experience, cultural traditions, genetic heritage, new information and analysis and synthesis. Most companies emphasize the fifth phase—data analysis, strategic planning,

MBA-style frameworks—but Boyd insisted this is the least influential of them all. Analysis and synthesis describe how you process information, but the other three determine what information you even notice.

Cultural traditions tell you what behaviors are rewarded, and which are punished in specific cultures. Genetic heritage influences your risk tolerance, your threat perception, and your stress responses. Prior experience—Boyd's most treacherous filter—creates an internal database of analogies, shortcuts, and instincts that whisper, "You've been here before," even when you haven't. Prior experience is how founders become overconfident, surgeons become pilots, and highly intelligent people fly straight into mountains. New information is of course, what you saw in the previous step of Observe.

And because these filters operate mostly subconsciously, they don't announce themselves. Instead, they shape the narrative inside your head, giving you the illusion of objectivity while quietly editing reality.

The impression of reality is the danger. And that's what my Antminer moment taught me far too late: that a founder's biggest blind spots are rarely information problems. They are Orientation problems—places where your internal story blocks you from noticing something obvious. Where biases put blinders on you.

Thomas, by contrast, learned this lesson in a much gentler way. His kitchen-table revelation was an early front-row seat to Boyd's theory: the surgeons weren't failing at patient care because they lacked skill or compassion; they were failing because their Orientation had been hijacked by a system that rewarded hierarchy over patient outcomes. Their worldview was a product of cultural traditions and institutional incentives, reinforced by years of prior experience, basically it was an Orientation toward politics. This was a perfectly logical Orientation inside the hospital—but a disastrously misaligned one outside it.

To truly understand the power of the Orientation system, you have to look closer at the Analysis and Synthesis filter, the last of the four categories. Most people, especially in business, think the fourth point is the whole game. They believe that if they just gather enough data (Analysis) and put it into a model or AI (Synthesis), the right answer will pop out. This is the fatal flaw of a rational person. Boyd, a fighter pilot, knew better. You as a founder should know better too. Boyd knew that the world is too fast, too messy, and too unpredictable for static models. His name for this process of changing one item or model into another, is called "Destruction and Creation"—the constant tearing down of old concepts and taking some old parts and adding new ideas to birth something totally new.

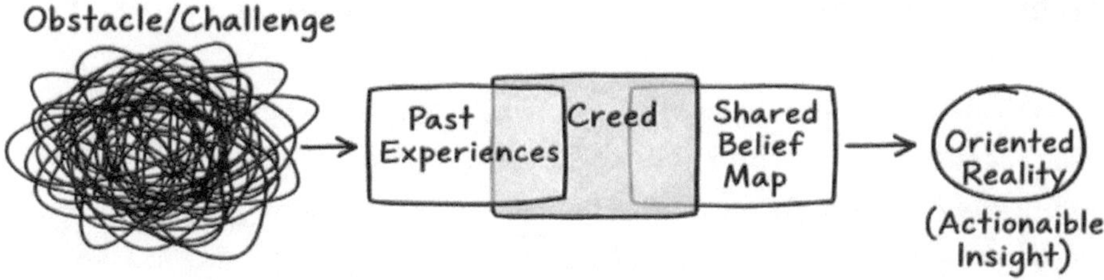

Figure 18—The BOODA Doctrine and your Team's combined history are how you find the way through the Gap.

The problem for the surgeons at Thomas's kitchen table wasn't a lack of skill or heart—it was the system that shaped them. Years of hierarchy, ingrained incentives, and institutional dogma had conditioned their attention to flow in one direction. The cultural traditions of the hospital, the professional pride born from mastering complex procedures, and the success metrics tied to political standing had combined like all the colors of the rainbow into a single, systemic black hole. The machine around them had created a monoculture of Orientation. Everyone was looking through the same narrow lens—one built to preserve the institution rather than to serve the patient. To use Earl Miller's metaphor, the spotlight had been fixed on their own standing, when it should have been casting a floodlight across the entire ecosystem.

Finding this kind of fatal flaw is the ultimate competitive advantage for the founder: If you can Orient yourself to the true mission, while your competitor is Orienting to the flawed incentive system, you will always win. Thomas started from the end goal—his true mission: The best outcome possible for the patient. Then he worked backwards focused on first principles and only built "must-haves," not nice to haves. Like every great founder he focused on one or two goals with tunnel vision.

This is the genetic heritage of the founder. It's the "on or off" switch, the "tunnel vision" that drives them forward. Thomas's Orientation was hardwired for simplicity and flow, a relentless focus on the goal. He hated waste, he hated noise, and he hated anything that disturbed the clear line between effort and result.

Orientation is best done by founders who can strip away the noise—the political system, the hierarchy, the doctor's God complex—and Orient solely to the value creation for the customer. **If you can't get down to the basic truths of the problem you are solving, you are likely spreading yourself too thin to hyper-scale.**

When Thomas started Nordic Health, he didn't try to fight the entire Danish healthcare system. He simply created his own version of a health system with a radically different Orientation. He talked to a traditional clinic in Malmö, Sweden that stopped surgeries at four o'clock in the afternoon. He asked the owner if he could use the surgery theater from four to eight at night. He offered the owner a share of every surgery he billed. It was found money for the clinic owner, so he said sure. Next, he heard about a talented vascular surgeon who would drive from Copenhagen home across the bridge to Malmö Sweden every day at four o'clock. He offered the doctor a percentage of every surgery if he would stop on his way home and perform very high-quality laser vascular surgery just on varicose veins. 30% of the world's population suffers from them Thomas reminded him, and surgeons don't like to do the simple but tedious procedure because it's not glamorous. Thomas showed him how it might not be sexy but if he was good, it could be very lucrative.

Figure 19—For founders true orientation means seeing past
the chaos to the customer at the core

"And then I'm thinking, you know, a clear, variable split for the doctors and the location. Simple, right? And it's aligned interest, every way, no fixed costs.

Super! I started advertising in the paper and the doctor was very happy when I had patients for him. All my costs were variable based on success; it was very different from the traditional way."

This wasn't a business model; it was a radical re-Orientation of the entire value chain. By aligning the incentives—the surgeon gets paid more for every patient, the clinic gets paid for unused time—Thomas created a system where everyone's Orientation was pointed directly at the customer. The patient's interest was no longer an afterthought; it was the engine of the entire business.

The established system, with its misaligned incentives, was slow, political, and inefficient. Thomas's rag-tag, variable-cost model was fast, simple, and hyper-efficient. He wasn't just competing on price; he was competing on rate of change, and he was winning because his Orientation was superior.

One of the greatest challenges for a successful founder is that their own Prior Experience becomes a trap. Thomas's success with his first, hyper-efficient, variable-cost clinics could have blinded him to the need for a diverse Orientation as the company scaled. He was lucky enough to have the curiosity that changed his world view. All of us are born to a certain family, that speaks a language (or two) specific to their culture, that lives in a specific geography, that has certain skin color, or house size, or traditions. These are the data influences that make up our subconscious mind, which executes our decision-making 80% of the time. If we stop to question a decision, it requires more energy - we use both hemispheres of our brain to analyze the decision, but that harder work means we decide of our own free will. When we challenge our subconscious decision, we can put new ideas into our subconscious mind. Doing that now, means that in the future, having an experience of putting new information into that database changes the past as we will see it in the future now subconsciously. This is how we can add to the depth of our Orientation, by changing our future past. It's a bit mind-bending I know, but important to think about.

Orientation is the gravitational center of the BOODA loop. It determines what information you notice and what you ignore. To stay curious and keep your lens from calcifying, you must institutionalize Boyd's idea of "Destruction and Creation"—the constant tearing down of old mental models to birth new ones.

As the founder, you are now at the point where you should become the Chief Dissonance Officer occasionally. Your job is to ensure the five filters of Orientation—Culture, Genetics, New Info, Experience, and Analysis-Synthesis

—are constantly challenged by your team. One of the best ways to do that is have a strong co-founder or founders and constantly challenge each other's blind spots.

The moment your team stops arguing, your Orientation has become a single, smooth channel—and that is exactly when you create your own new blind spot. Orientation is where you win the war before the first shot is ever fired. The more diversity in those strategic opinions the better. You want collision and argument. It requires the right chemistry to keep that momentum because it's often messy.

9

The Voltron Orientation

I.

If Chapter 8 was about the internal demons of the "Doctor Pilot," then Chapter 9 is about the construction of your co-pilot. I learned this lesson not in a boardroom, but on the back nine of a swanky golf club in Northern Virginia with the man who would become my co-founder at ServerVault. I spent the week before golfing with Jim Zinn doing what any founder with more ambition than skill does when meeting a potential investor on a golf course: I lived at the driving range like a pro-golfer with a huge gambling debt. Every evening, after doing my best to make heroic progress on the ServerVault business plan, finding our first data center space, chasing down used servers and looking for talented engineers; I drove to a strip of patchy turf that smelled faintly of fertilizer and regret. For about nine days I beat balls until my hands felt sandpapered. My mission wasn't to become a great golfer—just to avoid humiliating myself in front of the former CFO of the one of the largest credit card companies in the world, who was a keen angel investor. I got the intro through my attorney and I was going to make the most of it.

I didn't know Jim at all. I only knew the legend: disciplined, analytical, meticulous to a degree that bordered on supernatural. The kind of mind that could read a balance sheet like a cardiologist reads an EKG. When a man like that agrees to play golf with you, you try not to dig craters in the fairway, or drive your cart off the path into a water hazard.

Fortunately, the day I was to secure Jim as a key angel investor arrived and somehow, the golf gods smiled on me...at least for a while.

I took a few deep breaths as I stepped up to the first tee box. It was a straight-forward Par 4 so I teed off with a mostly-controllable four iron—right down the middle about 260 yards with a perfect roll. I raised my own eyebrows, that was a one in 20 shot for me. So it went, shot after shot. The front nine was the greatest golf of my life. Fairways, greens, a putting stroke that looked intentional rather than experimental. Inside, I was in disbelief, but I tried to project a relaxed and humble exterior. Jim watched with the calm detachment of someone who had seen real competence and didn't need to overreact to counterfeit versions of it. We were talking about server hosting, my vision of putting data "in the ether" on our computers for clients to access securely. I told him what we'd use the money for, and who we would hire. By the turn at the ninth green, we shook hands. His investment in ServerVault was now a promise and a handshake—I did it!

We were laughing and talking excitedly as we walked toward the 10th tee. I took a deep breath and smiled to myself. Just a couple strokes over par walking to the tee, I felt the natural, relaxed version of me coming back because it turned out Jim and I were hitting it off, really enjoying each other and talking openly and challenging beyond the superficial. He was a great guy, and I was lucky to have this time with him. Clearly something shifted inside me—quietly, but unmistakably. I wasn't pitching or performing any more, I was listening to the way Jim thought, the way he broke down risk, the way he Oriented to the world with almost forensic clarity. I realized I didn't merely want his check book; I wanted his perspective and guidance. His Orientation. His entire mental operating system, which was very different from mine. ServerVault didn't need more enthusiasm—it had dump trucks of mine. It needed the kind of mind that noticed what others missed and cared about the things I generally bulldozed past. That's when it hit me: he wasn't just an investor. He was the co-founder I needed.

Naturally, I did what every founder with too much adrenaline does: I began selling him on the idea before I'd even figured out how to say it gracefully. My enthusiasm spiked, my storytelling speed doubled, and in my excitement to convince him he was the missing piece... my golf game vanished. And I mean vanished. Poof!

One swing after playing like Rory McIlroy for nine holes, I turned into Rodney Dangerfield in Caddyshack. My drives zig-zagged across fairways. My irons tunneled into the earth like I was searching for oil. My putting stroke acquired the same erratic confidence as my 3-year-old nephew Charlie with a crayon. The back nine became a masterclass in athletic collapse. "That one got away from ya, Sweendawg." Jim deadpanned after one of my drives headed vaguely near the swimming pool 90 degrees and 100 yards away from the green.

But here's the critical difference—the one that belongs in this section of the book.

Jim didn't blink. He didn't flinch at the volatility. He didn't judge the chaos. He didn't get swept up in my energy or rattled by my unraveling. He simply Oriented differently and never stopped laughing or being positive. I had spent nine holes showing him my front-nine résumé with all my best points. The back nine revealed my operating reality and the dark side all of us founders have that sometimes off-sets the good stuff.

And Jim—steady, analytical, unshakable—didn't retreat from it. He leaned into it. Because the real test of a co-founder is not whether they're impressed by your best moments. It's whether they understand who you are in your least polished moments—and still see the value in joining you to cross that Belief Gap.

This is why the story belongs here, in Orientation.

The moment you know you've found the right co-founder is the moment your Orientations differ so completely that you each see solutions—and risks—the other cannot. Orientation isn't consensus; it's counter-point. It's two people studying the same situation and producing wildly different insights and realizing that those differences don't create friction. If you've got a Creed you both trust—those differences create lift. I teach founders the right co-founder is the one who stays calm when you morph into the worst version of yourself—the late-night, sleep-deprived goblin version who thinks a product pivot at 2:14 a.m. is a great idea. A co-founder is the person who notices the angles you blow past, who filters the noise you create without resenting the decibels, and whose mental model plugs directly into the gaps in yours like some weird entrepreneurial Voltron.[1]

---

[1]   Voltron is a fictional giant robot from an 1980s animated TV series. He was formed when five separate robotic lions combined into a single bad-ass warrior.

A true co-founder doesn't just help you cross the Belief Gap; they build the bridge from their side, knowing full well their worldview is not—and should never be—a carbon copy of yours. The magic is that neither of you can see the world the way the other does...and that's exactly the point.

II.

There's a second ingredient in the world-class co-founder recipe that founders chronically overlook: radical accountability. You hear a candidate say, "Traffic made me late... My boss had it out for me... I got totally screwed," and you might as well hear a submarine's dive siren. That's a victim mindset. Those aren't red flags—they're flare guns. A great co-founder owns their life, full stop. And sure, it's a bonus if they are already a friend, but only if you can look them dead in the eye and say, "You're wrong," and they don't crumble, pout, or call their therapist. They need your urgency, your ability to sacrifice, your willingness to sleep in your uncle's unheated garage if that's what the mission demands. Because when things get hard—and they always do—you can't have someone pulling what my COO at ODIN did and whispering "sayonara" as they quietly slip out the back door.

That day on the back nine with Jim was the moment ServerVault stopped being my vision and started becoming our company. The day Mr. Grumbles—who I introduced earlier in these pages—earned his place in the story. And the day I learned one of the deepest truths of Orientation: If you and your co-founder see the world the same way, you don't have a co-founder. You have a mirror. But a different Orientation—a complementary, stabilizing, Belief-expanding one—is just what you need. I had the big picture, the vison, the story-telling. I blew right by things like regulations, compliance, auditing, GAAP. The truth is if we didn't pay attention to those things we would have imploded when we became successful. And I needed a co-founder who saw what I didn't. That was Jimbo. And that's why he became my co-founder. I only wish I had him at DaVinci because he would have read that Antminer warranty cover to cover in his first week. Keep that in mind when you're starting your company.

Now, there is a nuance here which is critical that you understand. When I say Jim and I had different Orientations, I mean we processed and filtered data differently—he saw risk, I saw opportunity. He saw spreadsheets, I saw stories.

The nuance is that you have to be careful not to confuse "complementary skills" with "conflicting souls." The most successful co-founding pairs—like Pete and Sami at Trulia, or Brian and Joe at AirbnB, share a deeply similar worldview. They need to be able to finish each other's sentences on the big stuff, on the things that really matter. Like me and Jim, they had the same values and lived by the same creed.

If Jim and I had different values—if he wanted a quick flip and I wanted a legacy, or if he treated people like a cog in the machine and I treated them like family—we would have imploded. You need different Orientation filters to see the entire mountain range and storm clouds, but you need an identical Creed to fly in the same direction. If you have to debate the mission every day, you aren't going to move fast enough to survive. But make no mistake about having a co-founder, there is a lot of data that shows having two founders dramatically increases your startup's chance of becoming a Unicorn. In fact 80% of Unicorns are founded by two or more founders.[2]

Something else tends to happen at this exact stage of a company's life, and it almost always goes unnoticed at the time.

III.

Remember when you sold your first product or raised your first dollar? The press release goes out. The logo slide gets longer. And suddenly, you, the founder, are no longer the only adult in the room. This is when you are in danger of getting caught in the "Maturity Trap." As you scale and raise capital, new board members appear with impressive credentials from places like Goldman Sachs or IBM. They have opinions, but they haven't built a company from ten people to one hundred in a decade, maybe not ever.

Belief has weight. When you add voices optimized for risk mitigation rather than velocity, the center of gravity shifts. Cadence drops. Decisions take longer. From the outside, it looks like "growing up". From the inside, it's the moment your Belief gets diluted by well-intentioned interference.

Protect your speed. Protect your conviction. The best Orientation means nothing if the team hesitates at the threshold of Action. It's not easy to notice, because nothing dramatic breaks. No one storms out. The company doesn't implode.

It just... slows.

---

2   Defiance Capital study of 2,000 Unicorn founders. https://www.entrepreneur.com/business-news/unicorn-founders-have-three-simple-things-in-common-study/471772#:~:text=Founder%20teams%20were%20more%20common,valuation%20with%20their%20unicorn%20startup.

From the outside, this looks like maturity. From the inside, it feels like progress. It's often the moment Belief gets diluted—not by malice or incompetence, but by well-intentioned interference.

The best founders eventually learn to draw a hard line with board members. Not because boards are unhelpful, but because Belief, once dispersed, is hard to reassemble. Great boards at this stage understand their role intuitively: protect speed, protect conviction, and stay out of the way.

The ones that don't realize they should get out of the way and let the Pit Crew sprint; rarely notice the damage they are doing. By the time the damage shows up in the numbers, the moment is often gone and the chance to win the race has disappeared.

IV.

As Nordic Health Group grew, Thomas realized he needed to institutionalize their rag-tag advantage. He needed to ensure that the company's collective Orientation remained simple, focused, and free of the political noise that had corrupted the hospital system he grew up observing.

You can think of a successful adoption of the Orientation phase as a meritocracy of the misfits. Early on, when it was difficult to find surgeons, Thomas considered involving some of them as managers or even co-founders. However, it soon became clear that management roles were not the right fit for them, as the strengths of skilled surgeons lie in medicine not business operations. Their expertise and passion are best applied to the clinical field, while the demands and dynamics of running a business require a different focus and mindset. And for them personally, their management salary could never match what they could earn in the operating theatre, so it created an inherent misalignment of interests. Instead, Thomas oriented based on his experience, year at the dinner table, years working in private equity, years growing companies. He trusted his instinct that everyone should focus on what they do best. This meant relieving surgeons of all administrative responsibilities, allowing them to concentrate fully on patient care.

The solution was a deliberate embrace of cognitive diversity—the idea that the best team is not one of clones, but one of complementary, often contradictory, worldviews. Thomas needed people whose cultural traditions and prior experience would force him to look at the problem from an entirely new angle.

He hired people who were the opposite of the surgeon-manager. One of his early hires was a person whose Orientation is purely financial, a young analyst he met while working at a private equity fund before starting Nordic Health. He was a kid who sees the business as a series of levers and metrics, stripping away the emotional attachment of the founder.

"If you have a group of big brains that are constantly surprising each other because they are not aligned with the shared belief map (SBM) that's when you start losing key employees, dropping the ball on customers and missing key objectives," Thomas warned.

The key to keeping the team high-performing is that their dissent must be Orienting toward the same Belief—in Nordic's world the mission of patient value. It's not a democracy; it's a meritocracy of ideas, where the best idea wins, regardless of who presented it or how long they've been on the team. The surgeon's opinion on a new marketing strategy is judged on its merit, not by his title. The financial analyst's opinion on a new surgical technique is not immediately dismissed because he's not a doctor.

I mentioned the founder's job in the Orientation phase is to be the Chief Dissonance Officer too. It is your job to ensure that the filters of Orientation are being challenged by the most diverse, rag-tag group of brilliant misfits you can find.

But how do you, the founder, deliberately manipulate this phase to ensure your team's collective Orientation remains sharp, focused, and free of the V-Tail Doctor Killer's blind spot?

The answer is a deliberate, daily practice of Dissonance and Alignment.

1.   **Hire for the Blind Spot, Not the Resume**

The first and most critical piece of advice is to stop hiring people who look like you, talk like you, and think like you. You must hire for your Blind Spot. For many founders that is a technical genius who has an insane level of Belief in his or her own abilities to build something that's never been built before. Finding that courageous tech star dramatically increases your likelihood of success.

If your company is full of engineers, your blind spot is the customer's emotional journey. You need a poet. If your company is full of marketers, your blind spot is financial discipline. You need a former private equity analyst who sees the world as a series of cold, hard levers.

Thomas Lawaetz didn't just hire a business manager; he hired people who fundamentally challenged the Prior Experience and Cultural Traditions of the medical world. He brought in the financial analyst to tear down the emotional attachment to inefficient processes and the military strategist to tear down the hierarchy. Your job is to identify the dominant, successful Orientation in your company and hire its antithesis.

2.   Institutionalize the "Destruction and Creation" of Models

John Boyd has a concept of Destruction and Creation that is not just a theoretical exercise; it's a process you can institutionalize. Every quarter, your team must formally dedicate time to tearing down the models that made you successful. A couple exercises I do with startups that have just received their Series A or B funding and work well are the: "What If We Were Starting Today?" Exercise: Force your team to assume a competitor has just launched an identical product with 10x the funding. What assumptions would you destroy? What new model would you create?

And the "Enemy's Playbook" Review: Instead of reviewing your own success, review the success of your competitor. Be brutally honest. Don't just analyze what they did; try to Orient yourself to why they did it. What is their core belief? What is their blind spot? By stepping into their worldview, you sharpen your own. This practice ensures that your Analysis and Synthesis filter remains fluid, preventing your Prior Experience from becoming a cage.

3.   The Chief Dissonance Officer (CDO) Mandate

As the Chief Dissonance Officer your job is not to provide the right answers, but to ensure the right questions are being asked by the right people.

Elevate the Misfit: When the consensus is 9-to-1, your job is to give the one dissenting voice the floor and let her explain why she disagrees. Then force the other nine to articulate their Orientation to the lone dissenter. This is not about being difficult; it's about forcing the entire team to fully articulate their implicit guide for action—the mental model they are using to make decisions.

Then align the dissonance: The dissent must be focused on the Belief Gap you're crossing. The argument should never be about who is right, but about what best serves the mission, and the rocks your team is focused on. Thomas's team argued about how to deliver patient value, not if they should, because their Core Belief was all about delivering the best quality patient experience possible—no need to even think about what is most important. This is the difference between productive Orientation and destructive politics.

The Belief Gap—and the distance between your future vision and your team's current execution—is often just a gap in Orientation. When your team's worldview is aligned with the Creed, the execution becomes effortless. You are no longer managing a business; you are leading a movement. And that, my friend, is the only way to build a company that doesn't just win the battle but wins the war.

Thomas's entire journey, from the kitchen table revelation to the hyper-efficient Nordic Health Group, is a masterclass in superior Orientation. He saw that the established system was Orienting itself to the wrong thing: internal politics and self-interest. He chose to Orient his entire company to the right thing: patient value and aligned incentives.

The lasting lesson of Orientation is that you must constantly seek to destroy your own mental models before the market does it for you. The moment you become comfortable, the moment your team stops arguing, the moment your Orientation becomes a single, smooth channel, you have created your own blind spot. Perfect Orientation is not a destination; it is a launchpad. You've built your Voltron. You have the visionary who sees the future and the "Mr. Grumbles" who sees the fine print. You have a team that argues passionately but shares the same Creed.

In Kendall Square, a few blocks from the MIT labs where we studied the cost of task-switching, there's a saying: "Shipping is a feature". To reach Unicorn status, you must accept that your final Orientation will always be slightly blurry. You don't need a clear sky to fly; you just need to trust your instruments enough to Decide and Act immediately.

10

Decide – The Clarity of Conviction

Anja sighed.

Her shoulders, ramrod straight during her presentation, slumped a fraction of an inch. It was a tiny movement, but on the gallery screen of the Nordic Health Group's leadership Zoom call, it was as loud as a slamming door. The group, a constellation of Thomas Lawaetz's top executives staring back from five different countries, was suddenly as silent as a morgue.

They were discussing the German opportunity I mentioned earlier. Possibly the next beachhead in Nordic Health Group's march to 400 clinics. A country with a huge untapped market that they didn't yet occupy. Anja, his brilliant Operations Manager, had just finished presenting a detailed, data-backed plan for the first clinic location in Hamburg. All the numbers worked. The demographic analysis was sound. The financial models were solid. But there was a twist and it was eating him up.

And now, silence. The heavy, palpable silence of a team waiting for a decision that wasn't coming. It was at the same time awkward and disappointing, and

Thomas avoided the obvious.

The founder who once thrived on putting out fires and deciding, cleared his throat. "This is good, Anja. Really good," he began, the preamble to a 'but' everyone could feel coming. "But are we sure about the patient acquisition cost model? Can we get another analysis on the competitive landscape? I also need to model how we get the hospital two million euros a year out of the red. Can you dig in some more and circle back next week?"

He saw the flicker of frustration on their faces. His A-players weren't looking for that old firefighter anymore; they were looking for a flight controller to clear them for takeoff, and the tower just shut down.

In that moment, Thomas was staring down a problem he couldn't yet name, but its ghost haunted the digital graveyard of Silicon Valley.

What his team didn't know was that Thomas's hesitation over Hamburg was the aftershock of a much bigger earthquake. The twist I mentioned earlier. The real "freeze" had happened six months earlier. The German market, with its low competition and outdated methods, was a massive opportunity. But that piece of bureaucratic barbed wire coiled around the prize: to open a chain of vein clinics, "you had to own a hospital" kept him second-guessing. Thomas had found that money-losing behemoth, and a very willing private equity partner. The deal was on the table. All he had to do was sign.

Then his amygdala activated.

"That was a serious hesitation moment where I froze," he later admitted. "I figured all of our focus would be on the hospital, not on growing our network of clinics. It was losing two million dollars a year and I didn't know how to turn it around, but I would have to figure it out…It's something I've always done, you know, as the sole owner and founder, it's a little bit lonesome in decisions, especially when the whole company is counting on me."

To understand why a brilliant founder like Thomas would freeze, you have to look under the hood of the human brain. When you face a high-stakes decision, your amygdala—the brain's ancient warning system—lights up. It evolved to spot snakes in the water and lions in the grass, and to Thomas's amygdala, the uncertainty of buying a German hospital was a lion. As I explored in my book Fear is Fuel[1], the amygdala's fear reaction floods your system with cortisol and

---

[1]   Sweeney, P. J., II. (2020). *Fear is fuel: The surprising power to help you find purpose, passion, and performance.* Rowman & Littlefield.

adrenaline, hijacking your decision-making circuitry. It's the neurological basis for the imposter syndrome that creeps in when you're on the high wire, the feeling that one wrong move will expose you as a fraud. Thomas's request for "more data" wasn't a strategic query; it was his amygdala screaming for a certainty that doesn't exist. He was hiding from the lion.

After another week of stalling, he called me to bounce some ideas around. However, we quickly stopped talking about business strategy, because I could hear the stress in his voice. I made him breathe. I had him do a simple 4x4 breathing exercise over the phone. Inhale for four, hold for four, exhale for four, hold for four.

"What was that for?" Thomas asked, his voice already calmer.

"You're trying to fight a lion with a spreadsheet," I told him. "The problem isn't the data. You have to calm the lion before you can see the right path." As Yoda-like as this may sound it's pure Karl Friston—Thomas was facing that uncertainty and producing Free Energy that was causing him to freeze, classic analysis paralysis. The4x4 breathing works because the bottom-up input to his brain was that he was breathing calmly so he must not be in danger. With new information the brain gives the order to "shut off the amygdala."

He was quiet for a moment after this Jedi knowledge drop. "So how do I stop seeing lions?"

"You don't," I replied. "You just reframe the encounter. You need a creed for decisions, a way to turn threats into information."

The idea of reframing was the principle Thomas sorely lacked. The Hamburg clinic wasn't a single, life-or-death decision; it was the first data point in the next 346-clinic experiment. Choosing the "wrong" neighborhood wasn't a catastrophe; it was an incredibly valuable lesson for the next twenty locations. This attitude— that there are no failures, only outcomes that produce information—is what separates founders who get paralyzed from founders who get learning.

Acting with the goal of collecting data and not judging outcomes was the principal Thomas needed. The Hamburg clinic wasn't a single, life-or-death decision, but he was treating it like it was. It was the first data point in a 346-clinic experiment to get to 400. Choosing the "wrong" neighborhood wasn't a catastrophe; it was an incredibly valuable lesson for the next ten or twenty locations. They have enough cash to fund the clinic for 18 months—long enough to get great data and prove out any new hypothesis they might have.

The following Monday Thomas started his weekly executive Zoom call without asking for an update. Then he laid out a new principle for the company, borrowed from my experience at ServerVault and the 70% rule. "From now on," Thomas announced, "we will not wait for certainty. We will not let perfect be the enemy of done. **If we have what we believe is at least 70% of the available information, we decide, and we act."**

He paused, then looked directly at the square on his screen where Anja, his German Country Manager, was watching, her expression unreadable.

"Anja," he said, his voice firm with a conviction that had been absent for the past couple of weeks. "You have the plan. You have the data. You have more than 70% of the information. The decision to launch in Hamburg is no longer mine to make. It's yours. The tower is now open. You are cleared for takeoff. Let's talk next week about what data you've generated and what we can learn."

A new kind of silence fell over the call. It wasn't the lag of hesitation, but the stunned quiet of a new reality dawning. On Anja's face, a flicker of shock gave way to a slow, eyebrow raising, tooth revealing smile of pure determination. The firefighter had finally decided to become the air traffic controller. The question now hanging in the air was what his team would do with this new, terrifying freedom to act.

Thomas told me after his board call and meeting with some other CEOs in London he had an epiphany. "At first I hesitated, but realized that hesitation is only dangerous if it repeats... Friendster froze, but we built cadence through the BOODA Doctrine so we won't freeze again.

Cadence replaces chaos with the BOODA Doctrine.

From that priceless experience Thomas discovered one of the secrets to scaling at hyper-growth; speed of action. Even when things are calm and running well with very few fires to put out, speed is still king. The BOODA Doctrine is all about getting through the loops as quickly as possible and not freezing like Thomas did over Germany. It's always a sprint—if you have the structure in place then it's a sprint on a brand-new springy Olympic track. If you don't have a Doctrine and you try to build a company ad-hoc; it's like you're crawling over lava rocks. When you end up crawling, you realize you are the one responsible for the decision to try to sprint near a volcano.

II.

At ServerVault, we were dealing with customers from the Pentagon to Fortune 100 banks. Every meeting felt like a dress rehearsal for nuclear war. They were serious people, so serious, sadly, that all my hysterical dad jokes and Irish quips fell on deaf ears. In that environment, hesitation was the default. That kind of slow thinking tends to rub off on everyone, but I didn't want any of my employees at ServerVault to have that "that's the way we've always done it, don't rock the boat" mentality that's so prevalent in the world of big bureaucracies. It was up to me to make sure our team kept executing without fear of punishment or fear of making mistakes—we needed to move fast and break things, but beyond saying that and having banners hanging by the conference room what else could I say that would address the root issue?

We came up with an addition to our creed for decisions: **"There is no good news or bad news—only data."**

That single phrase reframed everything for our team at ServerVault. An engineer shipping code that broke something wasn't a failure; it was data. A sales pitch that fell flat wasn't a catastrophe; it was data. **And if every action, right or wrong, produces invaluable data, then the only true mistake is inaction.**

One bright sunny morning I was driving my beastly AMC H-1 Hummer down the George Washington Parkway to a meeting at the Pentagon for a new opportunity. The military guys loved to joke about my very pimped-out Humvee with posh leather interior and big sound system which I'd park next to the big armored versions whenever I could. My window was cracked and the crisp air reminded me that fall was coming. As I drove along, to my left was the hills of Maryland and a noticeably low aircraft coming down the Potomac into Reagan National Airport. I curved around the exit for the CIA (Langley) and was on the nicest part of the Parkway overlooking the river across to Georgetown's Campus and the Key Bridge. When suddenly directly in front of me I saw and heard and felt something I never thought I would experience in my lifetime. A mushroom cloud erupted from down the Parkway right at the site of the Pentagon. I ripped the steering wheel hard right to get onto Spout Run Parkway and head away from the Pentagon. I was terrifyingly sure a bomb just hit and there would likely be more. It was one of the few times in my life when my fear center was activated by a true threat to my life. The tragedy of 9/11 had a catastrophic impact on the world. I experienced it first-hand. In the aftermath and uncertainty days later, conflicting thoughts wrestled in my mind. I felt like driving back to rural New Hampshire and hunkering down in the woods or dropping everything to enlist and go get righteous retribution, but our company still needed to pay dozens of salaries, serve scores of clients and keep going. We did our best to keep up with our philosophy that there's no good news or bad news only data, but this hit home. It was beyond bad news. But we kept to our Creed and the attitude of separating emotion from data saved us after 9/11. While our competitors were holding meetings to strategize about the new demand for secure data centers and how to retrofit existing locations to be terrorist-proof, we were ahead of the pack, already acting, expanding our iron-clad model to a new facility in Dublin Ireland, and improving our security protocols. We generated real-world data, customers, and revenue while competitors were still analyzing hypotheticals

One of the paradoxes of decision-making is that the more you try to avoid mistakes or even hide them, the more likely you are to make fatal ones. Celebrate mistakes and tighten the Loop.

At dwinQ, the experiential marketing startup I founded, we literally baked mistakes into the process. We told teams: "Celebrate your mistakes." If a product demo glitched in front of a client, we didn't sweep it under the rug—we analyzed it, joked about it, and fixed it, usually within hours.

Why? Because mistakes are free data. They teach you faster than successes do.

The BOODA loop isn't about perfection. It's about velocity. Believe → Observe → Orient → Decide → Act, then repeat. The loop gets tighter every time you treat data—especially from mistakes—as fuel. If you penalize mistakes, your team slows down to analyze, blame and punish. If you celebrate them, you fix, and your team speeds up.

Punishing, analyzing, and blaming is where one particular ghost of Silicon Valley is most noticeable. It is the ghost of Friendster.

Back in 2003, Friendster was a unicorn before the term was coined, a first-mover social network so dominant Google tried to buy them—three times. But as the platform's architecture began to groan under the weight of its own success—pages loading with agonizing slowness—the leadership team did exactly what Thomas was doing. They hesitated. Thy didn't exactly freeze but they slowed a lot. Faced with the hard decision to overhaul their failing system and focus on one core product, they asked for more data. They tinkered. They spent more time filing patents than fixing the product. They were where Thomas was but on a global scale, asking for one more report. Meanwhile a scrappy Harvard side project called "TheFacebook" was governed by a creed that valued velocity over perfection: "Move fast and break things." With speed they eventually and easily relegated Friendster to the graveyard of wasted first-mover advantages. Friendster died not because its idea was bad, but because, like Thomas staring at his screen, they couldn't decide and act fast enough.

The breaking things is also where Friendster and Facebook diverged so dramatically. Friendster treated mistakes like shameful secrets. When load times stretched to twenty, thirty or forty seconds, the leadership hesitated. They wanted a perfect fix, and they feared being wrong. So they waited. Meanwhile, their users left.

Facebook didn't hesitate. They pushed imperfect code, broke features, and fixed them live. They moved fast because they believed that mistakes were not disasters—they were data. That difference in decision culture—fear versus speed— was the difference between becoming a footnote and becoming one of the most valuable companies in history.

III.

The difference between reckless speed and disciplined speed is your Creed.

When you have a Creed—a mission with a clearly articulated set of shared beliefs—you don't need to second-guess every choice. You don't need perfect information. You don't need unanimous votes.

At ServerVault, our Creed was built on security first, speed second. Every decision flowed from that. Did we spend extra money to fortify our facility? Yes, because security first. Did we sacrifice short-term margin to meet a compliance requirement? Yes, because security first.

Your Creed acts as a filter. It turns a thousand possible choices into a handful of obvious ones. And when you know your Creed, you can decide faster than your competitors who are still debating.

This is why Facebook could move at the speed it did. Zuckerberg's Creed was crystal clear: *connect the world*. That urgency overrode perfectionism. It justified "move fast and break things." And it turned imperfect product decisions into a coherent strategy.

Friendster, by contrast, had no such clarity. Their Creed was muddled: were they a social network, a gaming platform, a feature lab? Without that anchor, their decisions got slower, fuzzier, less consistent. They slowed, and the problem was they didn't have a Doctrine so they never unfroze; they got stuck in the Orient, and Decide stages. Nordic Health Group does have a Creed and they are now moving with clarity because they have the tools in place to decide and act quickly.

A founder without a Creed is like a pilot without instruments—every cloud looks like a storm, every decision feels like life or death. With a Creed, you have clarity and you have confidence and doubt is left to live in the house of your competitors.

Founders often imagine that the hardest decisions will be theirs alone—the lonely, 3 a.m. moments where you stare at the ceiling and wonder if you've lost your mind. That happens, of course. But in my experience, the most dangerous form of doubt isn't inside your own head. It's when doubt leaks into the team.

I've seen it at ServerVault, at dwinQ, and in almost every startup I've advised. It starts small. Someone questions whether the product roadmap is realistic. A board member pushes back on a funding ask. A customer churns. Suddenly, the team begins second-guessing not just the decision at hand but the entire direction of the company. This can be deadly.

This is where conviction has to be contagious, and curiosity directed. A founder's job isn't to have all the answers—it's to model decisiveness when everyone else hesitates. It's to manage the questioning with curiosity not judgement or fear. The language and the actions become critical when you, the founder, assign them.

One of the simplest rituals I created was a rule: we never autopsy a decision before it's acted on. In other words, no "paralysis by pre-mortem." Once we'd reached a 70% confidence threshold, we executed. Only afterward would we circle back to analyze and start a new loop. That small habit cut down on endless circular debates.

Doubt can also come from investors or partners who demand certainty. I remember sitting across from VCs we had just pitched for our Series A round. They wanted me to prove beyond any statistical doubt that a new automated security product would work 100% of the time. I said that's impossible and shortsighted. I reminded them of our 70% rule: make decisions with about 70% of the information you wish you had then act. Waiting for 90% or 100% certainty means you're already too late. We spent two hours talking about how we could achieve

99.999%. Despite what the VC wanted; we told them there is reasonable risk their demand was unattainable. We couldn't get that group to overcome their doubt. But that obstacle got us better prepared for our next pitch.

The reality is every founder faces skepticism. The great ones create systems that metabolize doubt into fuel. They don't let fear stall the loop. They codify rituals—decision thresholds, mistake celebrations, decision journals, "only data" mantras—that keep the company moving forward even when confidence wavers. This attitude has to start at the top with you.

Pete Flint, the co-founder of Trulia and now a General Partner at NFX, calls the end of the hesitation cycle the "F*ck It Moment." He sees it constantly with founders who have been hesitating for months—about firing a toxic sales leader, pivoting the product, or killing a feature. They wait and wait, paralyzed by the fear of being wrong, or the fear of loss.

Finally, they hit a wall. Maybe they have three months of cash left. Maybe a competitor just ate their lunch. The fear of death finally overrides the fear of making a mistake. They say, "F*ck it," and they make the move they knew they should have made six months ago.

And you know what? It usually works. The sacred cow gets slaughtered, the team rallies, and the company survives. But the tragedy is that they waited until their back was against the wall to trust their gut. They burned six months of runway buying "certainty" that never arrived, and missing the chance to collect new data to loop with the next time. Remember the only resource we can't get back? Time. The BOODA Doctrine is designed to bring that "F*ck It" clarity to a Tuesday morning stand-up months in advance, so you don't have to wait for the death rattle to decide.

Recognizing doubt is what Friendster never figured out. Their meetings became echo chambers of hesitation. Engineers knew performance issues were driving users away, but no one wanted to be the one to make a bold, imperfect call. Facebook, by contrast, metabolized doubt into speed. They institutionalized fast loops, knowing that conviction in action beats analysis in limbo.

IV.

If speed is so critical in this Orientation phase leading to Action how do you, as a founder, build this into your company? High-Velocity Decision-Making can have a framework within the BOODA Doctrine.

I've used the following with my own teams and with companies I advise:

1.   **Believe First.** Anchor decisions to your Creed. If a choice doesn't fit somewhere on your Shared Belief Map, it's noise and you shouldn't be wasting time on it. Make sure everyone in the company feels empowered to point out a mis-fit.

2.   **Bias to Action.** Assume action beats analysis. If you're 70% sure, Decide and Act.

3.   **Data Over Ego.** Don't protect your pride. Protect your loop. Every decision is data. As you scale this comes back to your hiring process, make sure you can determine if someone will admit quickly to being wrong and adopt the opposite position adamantly.

4.   **Celebrate Errors.** Make mistakes safe. Reward speed and learning over caution and delay. Celebrate the data you get back form mistakes, and remind the team long after.

5.   **Tighten the Loop.** Shorten the time between Decide and Act. Speed compounds. You need conviction to act fast, knowing it might not be the perfect decision but it will always create more data. Track the days or weeks it takes to move from the point of a decision to acting. Remember what Thomas learned **cadence replaces chaos with the BOODA— so go fast even when there are no fires, cadence first.**

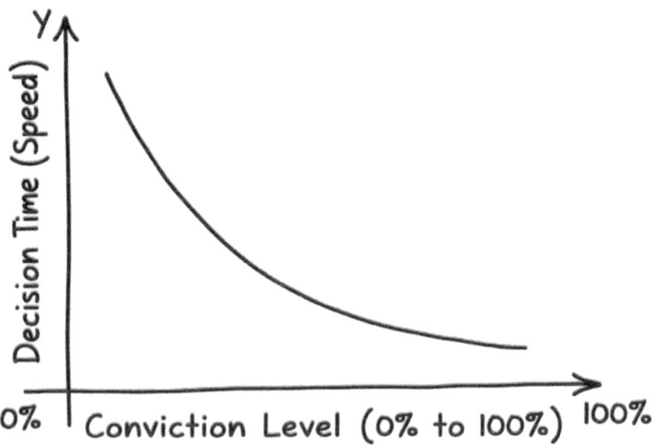

Figure 20—Anything you can do to speed up the loops is a bonus, conviction is at the top of the list.

This speed framework isn't theory—it's what separates unicorns from lifestyle businesses. Thomas adopted it and has weekly "BOODA meetings" that is their cadence. Facebook internalized it. Amazon codified it. ServerVault, ODIN and dwinQ lived it. Friendster ignored it, and now they're gone. Speed comes into play not just Deciding but Acting as well. There are two very different ways to Act ,though, kinetic and architectural and knowing which one you need to adopt can make all the difference in the world.

11

Act – The Relentless Pursuit of the Mission

I.

Factories at 3 a.m. are usually half-dead; Tesla's Fremont, California facility was throbbing like a Miami night club with a world-famous DJ just finding her flow. Fluorescents pressed every shadow flat; forklifts sang their backing vocals in reverse; clamped steel hit perfect notes when the press came down just right. Half-built Model 3s rolled on carriers like Buffalos mid-migration—hoods up, wiring harnesses draped across fenders, seats wrapped in plastic that crackled when you touched it. There are factories that run at night and factories that *live* at night. Fremont, in the summer of 2018, was alive, it was breathing Belief.

Elon Musk walked the line with the weary intensity of a battlefield surgeon. Wrinkled t-shirt. Red eyes. Hair tussled. He walked at a pace that made everyone else unconsciously quicken to keep up. He stopped at a robot cell that had jammed the entire line—some invisible electrical demon in a junction box that didn't want to cooperate. Elon listened to two engineers talk loudly over each other, then swung over the guardrail and climbed into the robotic cell himself. In Silicon

Valley, "founder-driven" usually means you still push code on the weekends. At Tesla it meant the CEO crawled under robots at 3 a.m. It also meant you could do something completely absurd and save the day, if you have a strong belief.

On the other side of the Belief Gap Tesla was crossing, the headlines were merciless: *production hell, cash burn, impossible targets.* Lots of obstacles. But the team inside the factory knew that those obstacles were the way—they believed they could overcome them and do the impossible. The promise of a $35,000 super-fast, electric car had pulled in nearly half a million deposits, like iron filings sucked to a magnet; now the filings seemed to be turning into neutered grains of sand in people's hands. The strategy and marketing were effective and elegant. The world was waiting. Decisions had been made. But decisions don't build cars. People, parts, and factory lines build cars—and this night, they weren't building anything because it was just too much demand for one facility.

Space within the building ran out. Inside, the choreography of high speed manufacturing had more elbows than room. Musk did the absurd thing every calm person first calls crazy and every operator later calls obvious: he ordered a tent. A gigantic, white, wedding-hall-from-Mars tent. From the road it looked like a something a bunch of carnies would hoist up for a county fair. Up close, what looked like the cotton-candy machine was in fact a laser-cutting machine slicing precision parts. A parallel assembly line grew outside the original factory beneath that canvas with borrowed equipment and hand-built fixtures. Musk built a field hospital for automobiles. Improvised? Absolutely. The thing about improvisation is that, while it's happening, outsiders can't tell genius from panic. You only learn the results after the fact, when the patient either walks out on her own or gets rolled out with a tag on her toe.

Factory folklore from that summer recounts the story of a pallet of brackets arriving two millimeters out of spec. Two millimeters is the size of a bit of pork barbeque stuck between your teeth in normal life, yet it is a week-killer in manu-facturing worlds. Musk Observed the miss. He Oriented on lead times, when he asked the supplier how long to get new brackets. Decided: we will save three days and ream the parts here, to spec, ourselves. Acted: they put a few vises on a bench, brought out drills out, hammers ready, and went to work. They had a flash-line of engineers, whose salary was enough to launch one of Musk's rockets, working like busy moms at a school bake sale. A couple hours later they were finished and the bottleneck moved somewhere else, which is all victory means in a factory. You don't conquer entropy; you nudge it along to the next spot.

This is one kind of Act: kinetic, sweaty, unfancy. Find the stuck point. Unstick it. Repeat five hundred times. No speech unjams a production line. No theory tightens a bolt. You can't *talk* about leading from the front. You go to the front. Leadership is often shown the way by the obstacle it faces.

Let's go halfway around the world now in the middle of a busy day. Thomas—the founder of Nordic Health Group—was *not* under a surgical lamp fixing a varicose vein rescue case. He was staring at a whiteboard that looked more tech startup than specialized hospital clinic. On one wall: a live map of clinics dotted with green and red beacons. On another: patient throughput numbers—first visit to diagnosis, diagnosis to treatment—numbers that breathed like a thoroughbred waiting in the starting gate. On a third: names—Single-Threaded Owners (STOs)—next to the outcomes they owned, each stamped with a date of last move like a passport.

Thomas's tent isn't canvas; it's protocol and education. His "secret weapon" is a living treatment playbook that operates like a private Wikipedia for surgery, he calls it Nordic Health Academy—it's the first stop every new surgeon and nurse makes when they join the Nordic Health team. It is a critical part of their Doctrine that not only helps indoctrinate the Belief, but that enables constant improvement and the highest quality care because very smart people are always trying to make the Academy better. Seventy-five surgeons don't just follow the rules; they challenge and update them, in public, where their peers can see. "If somebody has a best practice," he says, "they edit. Others challenge. We fight it out on paper before we ever fight it out on patients."

A creed without consequences is wall art. Nordic wired its Creed into compensation. Surgeons are paid only for successful treatments performed according to protocol. If a treatment fails, they redo it for free. If they deviate—say, a surgeon faces a challenge removing the vein with the laser and reverts to the traditional bailout with a scalpel opening up the patient—they don't get paid at all. Doctors have been removed from the team. Not because of politics. Because they were not humble. At Nordic Health Group, only the absolute best quality of treatment is accepted and if surgeon continues to perform sub-par they are replaced, simply because the interests of the patients are more important than anyone in the company. This is well thought-out, controlled, architected hygiene—it's a different way of acting from Tesla's kinetic action.

Two stories of two founders. Two acts. One in fire. One in calm. Same BOODA doctrine under the skin. Same search for speed.

Figure 21—The goal is always the same in Action - speed and precision.
They can be planned or reactions, both are appropriate.

By July, the tent, the ad-hoc stations, and the sleeplessness in Fremont produced one brutal fact: five thousand Model 3s in a single week. The obstacle showed them the way, but it didn't end the struggle. It put a bend in the curve. Momentum creates its own ecosystem: the temperamental production line starts producing; the hedging supplier commits; the doubting worker takes pride and is now a believer. The argument becomes an outcome of pure Belief because the founder delivered.

Meanwhile, in a Nordic Health clinic in Gothenburg Sweden, a surgeon faced a stubborn vein. Tissue spasmed. The old-school bailout—reach for a scalpel, open the patient, poke a hole, get it done—whispered its seductive shortcut. It was an obstacle with a traditional way of going around, avoid the obstacle and do it like it's always been done. Nordic's doctrine said no. The contract said no. The culture said: *learn the better way or go work somewhere else.* Yes, laser surgery working in three dimensions via an ultrasound is more difficult to master, but the surgeon joined the Nordic Health team because he believed in a better way. That day the surgeon stayed within the protocol and learned a trick from a colleague's edit (posted two days earlier): change the patient's angle, adjust the laser dwell time by a hair, avoid trauma. It took five minutes longer. The patient walked out without stitches, receiving the highest quality care in the industry.

Set the two scenes side by side and the lesson isn't Elon vs. Thomas. It's Elon *and* Thomas. In most companies crisis creates focus; calm invites drift and complacency. Musk's gift was acting in fire without burning down the ability to act later. Thomas's gift is acting fast in a state of calm—architecting a system where sprinting is the normal pace, not a reaction to sirens.

Thomas tours clinics like a curious student, not a general. "What did you change this week?" he asks. He's not making small talk; he's testing for a bias toward action. "Why did you change it?" he asks next. He's testing for ownership. If the answer is, "because the boss told me," something is broken. At ODIN I once fired an engineer who answered me with the line that makes my skin crawl when I asked why he did something the way he did—"That's how I've always done it." First time was forgivable, second time he was gone.

At Nordic Health, Thomas has a line he prefers to live rather than repeat. He said it once to me and then moved on, but I think it should be taught at business schools everywhere: "I'm trying to build a company where my most useful move is to stay out of the way." That's restraint as action.

II.

Founders love rooms with whiteboards because whiteboards are safe. I love whiteboards. You can draw the future and admire it. But the distance between planning and doing is where companies quietly die. Action creates feedback; feedback threatens identity to those not adopting the BOODA Doctrine. A decision on a whiteboard offends no one. A decision injected into the world tells you exactly where you're soft.

The mistake most founders make is staying Kinetic for too long. If you are still crawling under robots to fix a jam when you have 1,000 employees, you haven't built a company; you've built a high-stakes hobby that depends on your adrenaline. Or you are making a point. The transition to a Unicorn requires moving from Kinetic to Architectural Action for most of your work. You must move from solving the problem with your own sweat to solving the problem with a protocol—like the Nordic Health Academy—that allows 100 surgeons to solve it without you. This is how you widen your BOODA loop to encompass an entire organization.

The BOODA Doctrine doesn't indulge theater. Belief anchors direction.

Observe and Orient make sense of reality. Decide takes you to the edge. Act is when you put your foot onto the wire and take a deep breath. It's the only step the world can see. It's the only step that produces proprietary data. Your competitor can copy your slide deck. They cannot copy your week of learning and collecting new data on your hypothesis.

I drilled that one sentence into my teams at ServerVault, ODIN, dwinQ, and DaVinci 3.0 until they smirked and said it back to me: **There is no good news or bad news, only data. If a move "fails," you didn't fail—you paid tuition.** Hamburg, Germany didn't work out for Thomas, but the doctrine guarantees that the next ten clinics will be better and they'll be smarter because the learning is public across the entire company and therefore has value. It's not wasted effort that's whispered about in hallways.

Tesla's tent looked like chaos until you saw it as a speed lab. They weren't winging it; they were *compressing the distance between Decide and Act* so violently that the loop heated into insight. People call that heroism. It's hygiene—operational hygiene that keeps the loop clean and short. Act like you're shooting with one bullet left and you can't afford to miss. That's not bravado. That's prioritization turned kinetic.

On paper, I have eight plays I teach when the BOODA Doctrine workshop ends, and the rubber meets the road. On paper, it's easy for people to skim them. So let me tell you the plays the way they actually happen: as scenes.

At a very large company in Seattle, the hallways are lined with teams that share a product surface area but not a boss. Each outcome has a person's name next to it. Not a committee. Not a diffusion of responsibility hidden behind a clever acronym. A person. **When an outcome belongs to a person, decisions accelerate; when it belongs to a room, you send emails.** You don't need a million people to do this. You can do it with ten. The discipline is the same size at any size: pick an owner and let them own; this was a part of the genius of Jeff Bezos.

At Nordic, the STO board sits beside the map. You can stand five feet away and know, at a glance, which outcome is unloved: the one with the oldest last-move date. You don't need a sermon about accountability. You need a person's name next to her task and nothing falls through the cracks.

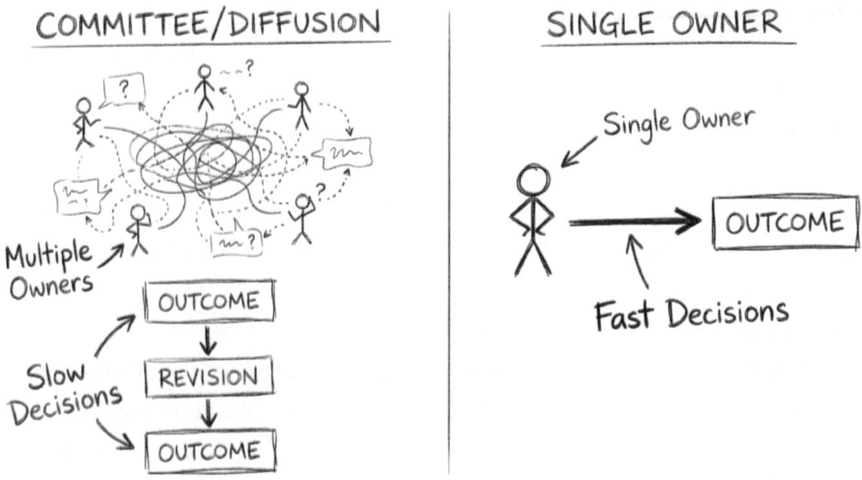

Figure 22—One owner eliminates noise and accelerates the BOODA Loop.

At the end of a strategy session the air feels caffeinated and virtuous. That's exactly when momentum can die—on the threshold between talk and touch. I ask one question: "What happens before noon tomorrow that reduces uncertainty?" Not "Design Version 2.0," which is a wish in a trench coat. Something with edges: "Shadow three new patients at Clinic X and time the identity verification step." We put a timestamp on it and book a five-minute check-in. If the move is too big for noon, the move is wrong. Momentum decays with each sunrise. Beat the sun. This is how John Boyd would fight entropy with his students. Do something now that is tangible.

Thomas did this after our first deep-dive. He wanted to standardize referrals across three countries. We didn't write a manifesto; he scheduled a ten-call sprint to the top-five sending physicians in Stockholm, Oslo, and Amsterdam. The script fit on a sticky note. By the second afternoon we had friction in our hands: Norway's privacy consent flow was the hidden choke point. Nobody in a conference room had even mentioned the privacy consent issue. The street mentioned it in five minutes, acting in the real world gave Thomas a key insight. BOODA gave him new data to adapt and loop again.

Operators are tempted by poetry—systemwide excellence, operating models, all that pretty language. Meanwhile a single part is stopping the line, or becoming the Herbie. The fastest way to freedom is to fix what's in the room with you. In

Fremont it was a bracket. At a Nordic Health clinic, it's an intake form question that burns for ninety seconds. In a software shop it's a flaky test that fails twice a week and opens a Slack storm. Find the narrowest choke. Clear it. Look for the next one. Repeat. Most companies try to boil an ocean when a kettle would do.

At Nordic, a clinic manager shortened intake by removing one redundant identity check. Ninety seconds a visit times 120 visits a day at his three clinics is three extra hours of care. No parade. No slide. A better Tuesday - let's do it again tomorrow.

If something is the bottleneck, put your best person on it as a STO and sprint. Don't wait for that friction to create fire.

If belief lives only in slide decks, you've built a religion for Belief Glut revivals. Instead bring the outside world in fast and listen carefully. I met the CIO of the US Secret Service at a conference, and he mentioned the desire to track handguns when they travel with the presidential motorcade across the country and work with local law enforcement. He also heard (rightly) that the physics of RFID wouldn't make it easy for him. I asked him to come to our lab and let us test out some ideas, "but full disclosure, Steve—we've never tracked a weapon." He said yes. He didn't think anyone had tracked guns yet, so no pressure. Early customer. Makeshift Lab. First users who don't owe us a compliment, and don't expect perfection because we told them not to.

At Nordic Health, they have a whiteboard to measure the outside world. It is not a museum piece in a quarterly review. It's on the wall where decisions are made. A red beacon on the map draws a small crowd the way a smoke alarm draws heads. Green beacons make Thomas smile. Someone owns it. Someone moves to get it green.

Urgency without edges becomes panic. Before it's too late to stop the melting snowball of burnt funding, install a kill switch. Decide what data stops the run or the new release. Decide what thresholds force a reset, make it concrete and definable like the blue line on an hockey rink. With your SBM, define the evidence that proves or disproves the thesis before you're in love with it. Bold action gets safer when everyone knows the experiment has a border, an edge, a guardrail.

Thomas learned this in the most pleasant way for a founder. A referral-flow change spiked throughput... and unexpected no-shows. Hitting the switch was pre-defined: a no-show rate over 15% for 30 days killed the test of the new referral-flow system. They punched the kill switch without a debate. Reset. Revise. Try something different. The team slept that night because the rule had been agreed while hearts and heads were cool, it's an extension of the second part of the BOODA Doctrine the Decision-Making Principles. But sometimes even the kill switch doesn't prevent colossal f*ck ups.

At ODIN we turned the most human emotion—embarrassment—into fuel. Once a month, at all-hands meeting, we handed a gold-spray-painted garden gnome to the team or leader whose mistake produced the most expensive insight. We called it the Golden Poop award. We brought the guilty party center stage. They told the story. We laughed. Then we wrote the lesson down—what we'd change, how we'd detect it earlier, where we'd put the tripwire next time. We had an entire wall made of white board coating in the lab where these lessons lived.

Our second year at ODIN we became the first company in the industry to use machine learning on RFID readers, and it gave us a massive advantage. No one had even heard of AI in 2003. Then with a handful of clients online and me feeling pretty good about my future, we shipped a firmware patch that made the readers hypersensitive to, what we called in the RFID world, cross-talk. In the lab it looked like magic; in the wild it was chaos. We started fixing it at five in the afternoon on Thursday and kept going for almost 40 hours. We lost a weekend but gained a blueprint for a field calibration protocol that saved future rollouts. In the 'Act' phase, the most expensive move isn't a mistake; it's an action without edges, like firing blanks. By installing Kill Switches and the Golden Poop award, you aren't just managing risk. You are lowering the activation energy of your team. When employees know exactly what data will stop a project, and that an expensive mistake will be applauded as a 'tuition payment,' they stop hesitating. They act with the speed of Belief because the fear of judgment has been removed from the loop. Removing judgement and shame starts with your charisma.

It's up to you, and your co-founders to get in front of your first 10 or 15 employees and recount the story of a recent mistake, and keep doing it for every new 10-20 employees. Just remember charisma is great until you're tired. That's when ritual works like it should. That's why you are reading the Founder's Creed to put that Doctrine to work. Thomas's BOODA meetings set the cadence for action. The meetings run eighteen to thirty minutes, anchored to outcomes and verbs: what we did, what we saw, what we learned, what we changed, and what we're doing today. No long oral book reports. No theater. Just movement and identifying friction, side by side. The rhythm is the boss even when the boss has had no sleep or is hung-over.

III.

If you want to *feel* action, go stand next to a physical production line. Making items you can touch is very different from software production, where faulty code hides traffic jams inside abstractions. Conveyors don't lie. When ODIN brought our first big healthcare customer into our lab in Ashburn, Virgina, I learned more in a week than most people would learn in three months of prototyping and modeling. Our RFID readers on conveyors didn't care about our hopes and dreams. They read what they read. We observed cross-talk reads— false greens lighting up for surgical kits on adjacent conveyors. To the client: alarming and exactly what you expected to happen; it created doubt in his mind. To me: it looked promising. It looked like data, I Believed in our ability to use that data. Loop again. We oriented on fields, antenna patterns, tag placement— the physics, not the pitch. The client was Johnson & Johnson and the leader of the group was a no-nonsense Boston guy named Dave. He wanted to verify every expensive part in a replacement joint surgical kit (knee, hip, etc.) to make sure surgeons received perfect kits ensuring a successful operation. Each kit was about the size of a roll-on suitcase. He was optimistic but at first, doubtful This is where my Belief and the Belief of our team saved the day. When we got 40-50% accuracy, we were pumped because it showed us what the problem was. We were actually excited to tackle this obstacle, our conviction was so concrete Dave could see it and feel it. He was starting to Believe. We decided to mock-up a Faraday tunnel for each surgical kit to go through to isolate the RF waves. We Acted—engineers bolting together aluminum frames like a pop-up ride at Disney's *It's a Small World*. The tunnel lengthened dwell time just enough to identify every piece inside. The rotating lights on each conveyor showed that greens meant "green" again. Johnson & Johnson sent us a plaque of thanks and we won some big industry awards for that solution. The better reward was the playbook we wrote the next morning when the coffee was still hot; we turned Belief into a second chance and found the way.

The field method is simple and effective:

Walk the assembly line (metaphorically or literally) once without speaking. Follow the object of value—car body, patient, replacement knee, ticket, then commit from start to finish. Watch handoffs. Note where things pile up. If you fix a problem with your words on the first pass, you will miss the thing that will embarrass you later.

Ask, "What work repeats?" Anything repeated is a candidate for early de-risking. Variability is the enemy of early execution because it makes every error feel new. Find the place where five minutes become five hours. Most production lines have gates; a few places with large consequences. For everyone who went to business school you probably read a book called The Goal.[1] It's a small book about a group of kids going on a hike and the fat kid slowing everyone down. They called the bottleneck "Herbie." Name yours. Babysit it and make sure someone is helping to carry his stuff and getting him in better shape.

Fix with a hammer, not a manifesto. If a bracket's too thick, shave it. If patient intake is bloated, delete a question. If customers drop at check-out do some testing, seat the person who knows "why" next to the break. If the tunnel can't read all tags, make the tunnel longer to increase the read field. Then move on.

Bottlenecks are whack-a-mole. You're not clearing the forest today; you're making a clearing you can work in. Tesla's tent wasn't a monument to flexibility; it was a knife. When the line jammed, they carved around the jam until a car rolled out the other side. That's what execution looks like when unfashionable verbs are in charge.

Addition feels industrious: one more initiative, one more OKR, one more metric. The courageous act after a decision is often subtraction. If everything is important, nothing is. If you can't name three things you'll stop funding, stop staffing, or stop reporting so the new decision can breathe, your decision is a wish dressed as a plan. Remember you only need 70% of the information to get to a great outcome if you Act.

If you are already a successful founder, you probably are tempted by adding-on already. You might be on the verge of hyper-growth. If so this amplifies the temptation to add new revenue streams. You raise money. The pressure to broaden is immediate—new markets, adjacent products, a dazzlingly obvious platform play. Maybe an acquisition or two. Entering a new category isn't an add-on. It's creating a whole new company with new SBMs, new channels, and a new failure profile. Expansion after a round is much more effort and often distraction than most founders think.

At ServerVault when we were adding our second data center I asked our CFO how much money we had for "good ideas while we're doing this hard thing."

---

1   Goldratt, Eliyahu M., and Jeff Cox. *The Goal: A Process of Ongoing Improvement.* North River Press, 1984

"None," he said. Perfect. That answer made us brave. We started saying the lines that make founders wince: "We're ignoring this auto-provisioning project for six weeks, while we get the network 99.99% in the new Dublin facility." "We're shipping uglier GUI on the new config page so we can ship something." "We're moving our best engineer off the beloved security product because the unloved provisioning one is the gate." Mr. Grumbles—Jimbo—took heat for canceling toys. That kept us alive.

If you want a crude, useful rule: two major projects, two rocks, per team per quarter. Everything else serves those rocks or waits its turn. Success makes cowardice expensive because you can afford to do many things badly. Act like you have a single bullet. Pick the target. Breathe. Squeeze the trigger.

IV.

People conflate urgency with recklessness. If you install guardrails on a curvy road, you are a lot more comfortable driving fast. In Washington, DC during my fellowship at the National War College, we spent a lot of time with the top military officers in the US, and NATO, talking about how to move quickly without breaking the wrong things, this is especially true for AI. When the guardrails finally clicked into place, speed followed naturally. The same logic holds at any company. Pre-commitment thresholds are the antidote to goalpost drift. Decide— up front—what metrics mean keep, pivot, or kill. Write them where everyone can see them, so future-you can't gaslight present-you into questioning your sanity.

Budget guardrails also turn prudence into empowerment. Give STOs money and time they can spend without new approvals. The founder who signs every invoice and calls it discipline is confusing Powerlifting with Pilates. Discipline is setting the budget envelope and watching what happens. This discipline can happen even when your company gets big and at risk of losing momentum.

As Trulia scaled toward their multi-billion-dollar exit, Pete and Sami realized they were slowing down. The main engine was getting heavy. To keep the speed of a startup while carrying the mass of a public company, they implemented a concept they called "Slingshots."

Inspired by the gravitational slingshot maneuvers used in space travel (serious geek reference, but both founders were physics majors in undergrad so it works), they broke the company down into half a dozen "startups within a startup." The goal wasn't just autonomy; it was acceleration. These small teams—consumer search, rentals, mortgage—were empowered to use the massive data and resources of the "mother ship" to slingshot themselves forward at velocities they couldn't achieve alone. This is the opposite of the Series A bloat that sirens founders into expanding in the wrong way.

They decentralized the execution but kept the Creed centralized. They realized that if you can move twice as fast as your opponent, you don't just win the turn; you become the Grandmaster. Trulia focused on making every single week 1% better than the last. That doesn't sound like much until you compound it over ten years of "Slingshot" maneuvers. That's how you outpace the market.

Guardrails don't slow you down. They relax that tension and stress squeezing your jaw and your shoulders so you can press the pedal harder, relax, and feel the road better.

Acting during a fire is easy; adrenaline sorts the list for you. The discipline is acting with the same clarity when nothing is on fire, that sets your cadence. Many founders become addicted to the righteousness of emergency. They structure their companies around their own heroics and then wonder why nobody moves unless flames are lighting up their ass. It's flattering. But it doesn't scale. Founders who want a legitimate shot at becoming a unicorn put in systems to scale. They let go of the flattery of their own heroics. Every founder who makes the 1-100 transition has to learn to delegate if they are going to scale with their company. Like Thomas said, he's doing his job well if he just stays out of the way.

You're a founder, you need to treat crisis like a class you attend once. Learn what Acting feels like at 120 hours a week. Drive that rhythm. Now, lose the martyrdom. Seventy hours is plenty. When doctrine is installed upstream, Act stops looking heroic and starts looking gravitational. Shared Belief makes movement cheap and fragmented Belief makes movement expensive. That's why Thomas spends more time on Creed than on calendar. Nordic isn't a democracy. It's a republic of owners, and republics only work when the constitution is legible, and a workshop or brainstorming session isn't the end game.

Workshops are intoxicating: clever matrices, new language, the pleasant ache of alignment. Then the consultants fly home, and the artifacts sit. The most important window in an initiative's life is the seventy-two hours after the decision. That's when momentum either appears or evaporates, you have the choice of Acting and increasing the rhythm of your BOODA loop or slowing it down. There's an easy way to keep the speed.

Hour zero to two is the commitment memo. One page. What we decided, why we decided it, the outcomes we're chasing, the risks we're accepting. Signed by the people with authority. Shared with the company. If you can't fit it on a page, you didn't decide—you discussed. That's why you need to time-box decisions, discussions slow down your loops.

Hour two to twenty-four is names and first moves. Outcomes receive owners. Owners commit to one discrete move with a timestamp. Not a wish. A move. What action will you Decide on and then Act the first day? Remember at MedXit they allocated 48 hours for A/B testing and finished in 24. Cadence.

Hour twenty-four to forty-eight is the dashboard. You should have enough information to put two to four KPIs in place that show real movement—throughput, defects, cycle time, dollars—posted where the work happens. The name and the number share a line.

Hour 48 to 72 is when you stop playing with whiteboards and throw your idea into traffic. One clinic. Ten users. Cut a mediocre vendor loose and see what breaks. You're not chasing victory—you're chasing friction. Because friction is truth. You want the market to punch you in the face fast, so your next move is built on evidence, not hope. Then you keep a cadence you can maintain when you're tired: short daily stand-ups; weekly BOODA debriefs that separate signal from noise; monthly resets where you kill projects on purpose. A company that never kills projects has forgotten how to decide.

V.

If you're reading this at 3 a.m., you're either living on fire or living in fear of calm. The fork in the road is simple enough to write on a napkin.

On one side is the Tesla Tent Moment. The line's jammed and it smells like shit—hot metal, sweat, frustration and melting plastic. Everyone's staring like the problem's going to fix itself. It won't. The smart move isn't fancy—in fact, it's ugly. Slam the part in a vise. Ream the damn hole. Hell, drag the line out into the parking lot under a tent if that's what it takes. Don't confuse looking clever with being effective. Act like you've only got one bullet left, and missing means you're dead.

On the other side is Surgical Restraint. Your jam is you. **You've become the hero under the lamp. It feels noble; but it turns you, the founder, into the bottleneck.** The doctrine you wrote is waiting for you to trust it. Let the system work. Let the doctor solve the case within the protocol and structure you designed. Ask your two questions—What did you change? Why did you change it?—then leave. Restraint becomes the Act.

With either path, the thesis is the same: Act so the world can't misunderstand your intent. Your final argument is the outcome, the obstacles you crossed.

One last walk through the Fremont factory. The tent hums—white, a little ridiculous, but very effective. Inside the main building, the dashboards look less like a heart monitor in the middle of a sprint and more like resting pulse on a leisurely walk. Somewhere, a new problem is brewing, a new obstacle; factories and companies and lives are made of new problems. Under the tent, the ground hums anyway.

Across the continent, in Gothenburg, patient intake shortens by two minutes because a nurse tried pre-filling out part of each form. She didn't ask permission. In Bergen, a clinic admin moves referrals from red to yellow because she has authority and the habit of movement, she Acts. Thomas won't let a surgeon move the referral because it's not what they do best. The STO board shows a row that was yellow yesterday and green this morning. Someone slept better last night than they did last week.

And then there's the corridor moment. A doctor stops Thomas on his way to the stairs. He's got a decade of surgeries under his belt, competent and careful, not prone to speeches. "Because of our doctrine," he says, almost sheepish, "I did more vein surgeries this week than I did in six months last year at the hospital—and the quality is higher. Your protocol forced me to get better. I'm faster and I'm safer. Thank you." Thomas nods, says something brief about the team, and keeps walking. It's not false modesty. It's cadence. The system is the hero, and the system is what trains the unicorn.

"We feel a great honor in being able to do one thing well." Stated Thomas, "It's almost a moral duty to scale it if you can, so more people can benefit." That is rock-solid Belief in what he is building.

In some distant place you've never heard of, a founder just like you turns down an invite to another Venture Capital Conference and gets back to pushing a feature to staging instead. The team is waiting, and he is delivering. They're looping. Every loop changes a company. Every loop buys data your competitor won't have until they wake up. Most acts of hyper-growth startups aren't dramatic. They look like tents and reamed brackets and eight-minute stand-ups and awkward Friday emails that kill a project you loved. They look like work. The only way that a Doctrine can become magic is through the work.

Your final argument is the outcome you produce. Make your future and success impossible to misunderstand.

12

From Creed to Legacy

I.

The news rumbled through the company like a small, quiet earthquake. At Patagonia's headquarters in Ventura, California, people looked up from their laptops and needed to validate what they just saw on their email. Every inbox in the company just pinged with something from their founder. Subject line: Earth Is Our Only Shareholder.

For a long couple of minutes no one moved. A woman in accounting reread the line twice, whispering the words as if they might rearrange themselves into something ordinary. Does that mean what I think it means? She looked across her cubicle to see if others had seen it. A product designer laughed, a short disbelieving bark that turned into a laugh at the incredibility and audacity of what the email meant. Someone in the repair department—the group that stitched worn jackets and replaced zippers—started clapping and whooping. The normal buzz of chit-chat and machines was overcome by the blooming of collective astonishment.

Yvon Chouinard had done the unthinkable. He hadn't sold his company or taken it public. He didn't put it in his will for his two children to run. He had *given away a multi-billion dollar industry leader...to the world*. Chouinard folded its ownership into trusts so that every dollar not needed to keep the business alive

173

would fight to protect the planet that inspired it. It was the ultimate stroke of taking care of the environment; put your money where your mouth is.

Outside their offices, the surf rolled in as it always did. Inside, the staff tried to fathom what had just happened. There were no confetti cannons, no victory speech, just the deep, calm sense that the founder had finally taken their Creed, the idea born in Yosemite decades ago to its inevitable summit.

Three thousand miles away from Patagonia, a fluorescent light hummed above a classroom at the University of Virginia. That day was now over 25 years ago and I was a second-year student at the Darden School of Business sitting in one of my strategy classes. On the projector, a PowerPoint slide titled: Paths to Liquidity.

Underneath it four options:

IPO | Acquisition | Management Buyout | Merger.

I was sitting in a strategy class led by a very talented professor. "Every enterprise," he said, "needs an endgame." I heard him from my comfortable overwatch in the back row of the horseshoe shaped classroom. I was surrounded by the future of elite consultants and investment bankers, and the word *endgame* stuck in my throat. I raised my hand.

"What if there isn't one?" I asked. "What if a founder built something that was supposed to keep going—without an exit, without cashing out, like these eighth-generation shipping companies in Singapore?"

The professor blinked, as if I'd spoken another language.

"Eventually," he said, "everyone exits. Even if it's horizontally."

The room laughed.

The idea of building something just to maximize the value seemed to contrast with another course I took my second year at Darden which was taught by the Dean of UVA's architectural school, Will McDonough. He taught about sustainable design - we had case studies of how radical it was for BMW to design a car that is meant to be pulled apart at end of life and recycled and parts re-used. We learned about LEEDS certifications, and gray-water collection and grass roof-tops. It was a radical class for the late 1990s. The idea was building things to help the planet not just to maximize value. But in the strategy class I learned that in the grammar of business, verbs like *give* or *endure* rarely appear. The MBA dictionary seemed to start with *scale* and end with *liquidity*. Thankfully, top MBA programs have changed a lot over the last 25 years, and more founders are focused on purpose as well as profit.

Years after I graduated from UVA, in 2022, when news of Chouinard's move lit up my inbox, I thought of that Darden classroom. The brilliance of Chouinard's act wasn't rebellion; it was *consistency*. For fifty years he'd been sewing belief into every seam and product tag: stop selling pitons that scar rock, build jackets that last decades, advertise with the sincere warning *Don't Buy This Jacket* to fashionistas who wear clothes for one season and discard it for the new collection. What looked like marketing was Patagonia's Creed enhancing commerce. The postcard to the world was just the last, clean turn of the loop.

Now I understand what I couldn't articulate at Darden: a company can have an afterlife if its founder has the courage to replace ego with creed. Creed can eventually become soul.

Leave the California surf behind for a minute and let's go across the country to present-day Kendall Square. MedXit's engineers are arriving early, espresso steaming next to rows of monitors that glow with patient data. A line of code that began as an experiment months ago has just gone live across a dozen hospitals in Massachusetts. Nobody cuts a ribbon. The success metric is silence—no alarms, no crashes, only the steady rhythm of information moving through the system, learning as it goes.

And in Gothenburg, Thomas is already halfway through rounds of the Nordic Health clinic. He pauses outside an operating room where a young surgeon stands over a patient's leg, the laser poised above a difficult vein. The rule is clear: no scalpels, no shortcuts. The doctrine holds, even without Thomas in the room.

Their creeds have gone feral—in the best possible way.

Just as Chouinard's mountain logic infiltrated a billion-dollar brand, the BOODA Doctrine is now replicating inside hospitals and data centers. It's no longer philosophy; it's procedure for dozens, soon thousands of companies like yours. The question I once asked in that Darden classroom—*Can belief outlive the founder?*—is being tested in real time on living systems.

No one knows how these stories will end. That's the point. Legacy isn't an answer; it's a loop still cycling. As you've seen, the best companies keep their cadence and keep their foot pressed hard on the pedal.

II.

On a gray Tuesday in Kendall Square in Cambridge, the Massachusetts sky had the color of recycled paper and the mood inside MedXit wasn't much brighter.

From their perch in One Broadway they gazed across the Charles River to a grey-cast Citgo sign that looked as colorless as they felt. A line of code—five words, plus a missing semicolon—had taken away visibility to a cluster of patients from the hospital on Nantucket. The monitors still showed pulse rates and blood-oxygen curves, but they were ghost numbers: stale, frozen, a snapshot in the moment of a life. Across the pond in Krakow Poland, three of their off-shore developers shared the same room, sitting shoulder to shoulder, eyes glazed from a non-stop twenty-hour coding effort. They were trading hypotheses in a low monotone Polish. One of them prayed in Python.

"F*ck!" Came the accented English from a junior developer named Rita, who pointed at a query-log scrolling like rain.

"There," she said. "It's not the data—it's the handshake between nodes."

The room stilled. An electronic handshake. Five seconds of silence and then the clatter of fingers pounding keys. Code unfurled. Within minutes, the first patients pinged back to life, metaphorically speaking. Rita leaned back, letting out a long whoosh of air, half-laughing as she did.

Her manager turned and said the line everyone in the company had learned from their founder:

"There is no good news or bad news, only data. Nice fix."

That sentence had traveled farther than I ever expected. It had become a kind of company prayer, muttered when the adrenaline hit too fast. MedXit's doctrine wasn't printed on pens or coffee mugs; **it lived in these moments when fear wanted to take the keyboard and Belief politely asked for it back.** At roughly the same hour, hundreds of miles north in Gothenburg, Thomas was fighting a different kind of gremlin.

In a third-floor operating theater of their clinic, a surgeon named Eva was staring at a vein that refused to cooperate. The vein spasmed under the laser insertion, slippery, almost mocking. The safe—tempting—alternative was go old school; open the leg with a scalpel. Every hospital in Europe would have blessed that course of action. But you already know their creed, so did she. Scalpel? Nope, not just one time. Not anyone, not anymore. Scalpels are not part of Nordic's creed.

Thomas stood behind the glass, hands in his pockets, saying nothing. The doctrine was clear: *laser or leave.* He watched her blink her eyes hard, breathe, blink again. The nurse glanced toward Thomas, silently asking for a nod he wouldn't give. Then Eva exhaled, shifted her angle, and the vein sealed in a perfect white line of light. The monitor beeped once and went still. Success.

Thomas didn't smile. He just nodded with a whispered to himself, "Good," and walked away.

The nurse bumped into him later in the company break room. He poured two cups of coffee and said to her, "Belief doesn't mean you never doubt. It means you doubt cleanly. Then you execute cleanly—that's operational hygiene."

By week's end the clinic's output data told its own story: procedures up eighteen percent, errors down to zero. The doctrine was performing surgery on itself, it created the highest quality care in the industry.

MedXit and Nordic Health were learning the same lesson Patagonia had mastered years earlier: when Belief plus your Creed becomes your operating system, the founder's voice turns into background music. You can hear it if you listen, but you don't need to.

At MedXit, dashboards began to look less like spreadsheets and more like pulse charts—breathing, adapting. The engineers started joking that the system had a personality: impatient but fair. It rewarded curiosity and punished sloppiness. Thomas's clinics felt the same way. The creed was quietly rewiring the people who practiced it. Belief is never a static asset. It drifts, it mutates, it begs to be proven again. The obstacles and the people on the other side of the Belief Gap will test you. And they'll test your team. They can't yet see the future you are already living in, so they challenge it. Vision is one of your super-powers as a founder. Every doctrine, no matter how elegant, eventually meets its storm.

Both companies faced their own storms; predictable for hyper-growth success stories. The storm arrived in the form of scale. MedXit signed a deal with a massive public-health consortium in Worchester, Mass—thousands of new data feeds, tens of thousands of patients. Investors cheered. The founders took a breath. Thomas, meanwhile, opened his fifty-fifth clinic and started training the next generation of surgeons who hadn't grown up inside the culture living their creed. As he recruited, he saw hesitation in their eyes: their instinct was they wanted to follow the rulebook, not a Creed. A system that once felt alive risked calcifying into compliance. Their BOODA doctrine was about to find out whether it could breathe on its own.

III.

Years earlier, I was on a plane somewhere between Boston and Moscow, watching clouds bunch like cotton balls below the wing. I'd spent months teaching a small group of founders how to act without being the bottleneck, without needing my guidance or any board guidance, and now I caught myself wondering if the lesson would hold in the years ahead. Chouinard's gift to the planet had been faith and belief disguised as structure. Could I give founders the same thing—something that would outlast their presence and mine? As this was playing through my mind the seatbelt sign pinged on and the captain announced turbulence for the next 30 minutes or so. I smiled at the timing. The Universe has a sense of humor with me and always will. What happens when your creed hits inclement weather? That's the question every founder eventually answers not in theory but in practice.

In Eastern Russia, the wind on Europe's highest mountain, Mount Elbrus, sounds like a hissing snake at first, then like an argument among giants when it builds up. It sneaks into your collar and down your spine, then finally convinces you that your bones are microphones recording the sound of cold. At 15,000 feet, the air is a rumor. Every breath is a negotiation you might lose to your lungs. I'd been here before — not on this ridge, maybe, but in this posture: bent forward, lungs on fire, muscles staging a mutiny while some small voice keeps saying *step, breathe, again.* The once light carbon fiber fat-bike strapped to my back is feeling like the weight of the world pulling me down. Yeah, there's a bike strapped to me.

Figure 23—That's your humble and somewhat daft author bringing a bike to the summit of Mt Elbrus, Europe's highest mountain for an exciting (and first ever) ride down.

There's a point in every climb where ambition stops being fuel and starts being more weight. Belief has to take over. You have to let go of the doubt and the negative image of the future.

The night before at high camp, the storm rolled in like a threat come true. The guides debated. The forecasts were unreadable noise. Our guide looked at me and said, "If we go now, it's not smart."

I laughed. "It's hardly ever smart. It's necessary. You and me and PJ will give the summit push a go. We will turn back if things get sketchy, or that southern air mass moves up." PJ was my 11-year-old son. Here's the back story - I was attempting to be the first person to climb Europe's highest mountain and then bike down. PJ joined me for the adventure on foot for the first half. Knowing I'd be significantly faster than him on the way down I hired a local guide to stay with him, so I knew he'd be safe after I started my shred down the roof of Europe. If all went well we'd meet up again at the high camp.

At 3:17 a.m. I roped up with PJ and the guide and we started up. The snow squeaked the way Styrofoam does when you pull it apart — a sound that makes your teeth ache. Somewhere behind me, a climber was coughing through his balaclava. Headlamps bobbed like uncertain stars in little constellations of clients and guides—three or four behind us, by a few hundred yards, six or eight ahead of and above us spread out over a half mile. It was a scene I had experienced on dozens of peaks around the world. The cadence was always the same.

Step.
Breathe.
Repeat.

There's no philosophy at that hour, at that altitude, just physics and will. But if you stay long enough in that narrow rhythm, you begin to hear echoes of every creed you've ever believed.

Believe. Observe. Orient. Decide. Act. It's not a slogan in the cold; it's the oxygen you need to move.

Halfway up, the visibility dropped to ten yards. The world became a tunnel of white. I could no longer tell if I was moving or if the mountain was. One slip of depth perception and I'd be a cautionary tale told over beer by guides who'd never learn my name. **So I did what the BOODA Doctrine teaches: I tightened the loop. I stopped thinking in hours and miles. I started thinking in moments and yards.** Observe: snowdrift curling east. Orient: the rope tugs north. Decide: left foot. Act: lift and step. I just need ten more left and rights. Then ten more again. Break it into bite size moments.

"Dad?" PJ's voice snapped me out of the flow. "My feet are really cold." We were at least two hours from the summit at our pace. PJ was very fit—we'd climbed a bunch of 14,000 footers in Colorado as part of our training during the months leading up to this adventure. He'd practiced self-arrest and using the ice ax to belay. He was ready. But he chose lighter climbing boots which worked great in the summer of Colorado. Now he was learning the tradeoff in harsh reality—lighter equals faster, and lighter also equals colder. With a heavy heart, full of disappointment, he decided to turn back to high camp. He and the guide left me, the guide warned me to follow the small flags other guides stuck in the snow to help avoid cliffs and crevasses. The markers he mentioned reminded me of the flags we used to train our dog on the electric fence; go past them and you get a shock. A big shock. I went back to march mode. I went to looking and thinking and stepping and doing it again. Now I was alone.

The loop shrank until it was nothing but heartbeat and motion. And then, without ceremony, the sky came to meet me. The thirty yards of visibility shrunk to zero. I couldn't find the little flags anymore but kept inching up trying to maintain the same direction. I knew I was less than 100 yards from the summit. But I knew it could be a deadly 100 yards. The clouds swirled around me like smoke. The summit revealed itself not as a victory but as a mercy — the end of uncertainty. I said a prayer of gratitude and turned to put the wheel on my bike and walk down to where I could see the flags again and ride with confidence. I didn't raise my arms or shout. I just looked out at the endless white and thought about PJ. Then I thought about the young founders I was working with and I realized they were all climbing their own ridges, tightening their own loops, breathing belief through bad weather and zero visibility. I remembered that familiar feeling of fear.

I have these moments often in the mountains, my ideas gelling or reinforcing themselves in my mind. This time it was philosophic: Belief doesn't scale by being shouted. The rah-rah noise of companies like Enron is just that; noise. Belief comes from a strong signal, and it scales by being practiced. **The BOODA Doctrine is your choreography learned in calm, so it works in chaos.**

Back on the mountain, ripping an incredible decent on my fat bike, laughing like a simpleton across snowfields and glaciers; I passed several teams of climbers still going up. I was having the most fun I could image riding my carbon-framed bike down Europe's highest mountain. The climbers were gray with exhaustion but then their eyes lit up in wonder to see a man screaming down on a bicycle from one of the Seven Summits. If someone asked them before they started their climb; "You think they'll be anyone biking down Elbrus today?" they would have been firmly on the other side of the Belief Gap—"What? No way, are you crazy? That's impossible. Why would they?" And my answer would be to ask Philipe Petit.

Later, when I was back in the metal barrel-shaped hut, shaking from the inside out, I remembered something a US Navy Admiral once told me: **"Restraint is a form of motion too."** Acting doesn't always mean pushing harder. Sometimes it means holding still until the signal is clear. This is a very tough balance that, like the right amount of reverb in a guitar solo, is only learned through practice and presence. Fast-forward a few years to today in Chamonix. I opened my inbox to find two messages waiting. The first was from Thomas. A short text: *Back from holidays, no calls. The system ran a week without me. Better than before!*

The second was from MedXit's CTO. No punctuation, just relief: *The new AI learned how to self-correct the Doctor's report. It didn't even wake us up this time. The system we built is incredible.*

I chuckled with satisfaction. The doctrine was outgrowing its authors. The loops were alive. That's what this whole journey has been about — the companies, the climbs, the sleepless nights in tents and factories and labs and boardrooms. None of it was about control. It was about letting go. The point of Belief wasn't to hold on tighter; it was to build something that could move without you. Legacy isn't a summit; it's not a product or an award. It's the moment the system keeps climbing on its own.

The thing no one tells you about climbing summits is how loud the silence is on the way down. After the adrenaline fades and the chatter in your head dies, the only sound left is your own breathing backed by squeaking snow—but it's different now. The rhythm slows. The loop widens. The urgency that pushed you upward turns into something closer to gratitude.

On my way down from Elbrus by the time I reached high camp, the mountain had already erased my footprints and tire marks. PJ was warm and fed and was happy to see me back. That's the part most founders never expect: your work disappears faster than you think, and if you're lucky it has made someone happy and changed lives. But no matter what we do, eventually the world covers your tracks. And if you've done it right, it doesn't matter. The mountain still stands, and so does what you built.

I remembered that classroom at Darden—the hum of the projector, the professor clicking through slides, everyone nodding over exit strategies and EBITDA multiples as if life itself could be modeled in Excel. I'd asked the question that hung in the air like a flare that no one wanted to chase: *What if the point isn't to leave? What if it's to last?*

One of my professors, Jim Collins, tried to answer that years earlier with his own book—*Built to Last* the sequel to his best-seller *Good to Great*. But my version of the idea wasn't born in a lecture hall. It started in sawdust. Back in college, when I was running my little construction company, we were installing cedar plank siding on a new house in Keene, NH. Above the garage, I spent an extra day crafting a sunburst pattern out of cedar clapboards—just because it felt right. The client never asked for it, and it slowed the job down, but I wanted that house to have a fingerprint. That was thirty-five years ago. The house has changed owners a few times since, but whenever I'm in town visiting friends, I drive by. I look up and see that sunburst catching the light. Nobody knows who put it there. They don't have to. It's still doing its job—quietly outlasting me.

Back in Chamonix the air always feels sharper, as if it's been filtered through centuries of ambition and regret. The mountains don't care how much equity you own. They ask simpler questions: Do you believe? Can you move? Will you get up again when it hurts? Do you doubt yourself?

I walked through the narrow streets of town—past the patisserie with its fogged windows, past the alpinists sipping espresso out of chipped mugs. The sky was a hard blue that made the snow look like porcelain. Mont Blanc was half-hidden in cloud, a lenticular form the locals call a "Chapeau" for its resemblance to a French beret. The mountain's white shoulder jutted out below the cloud like a sleeping god under a giant blanket.

From somewhere above the Aiguille du Midi parking lot I could hear the whistle of wind from a speed rider on his miniature paraglider cutting across the sky, just a streak of color and courage. It reminded me how small belief starts— one person, one idea, one stubborn act that says, *this can be better.*

I stopped at the 4810 Café, named after the height of Mont Blanc in meters, the same place where I'd written parts of *Fear Is Fuel*. The waiter brought me a cappuccino and, without asking, a Pain au Chocolate. I smiled—this was France, after all. I pulled out my ragged Moleskin notebook, where I jot down random thoughts and observations, opened to a clean page, and wrote three words at the top: Believe. Act. Endure.

Then I thought about all the founders who might one day be reading these words—someone sitting in a half-lit office at two thirty in the morning, staring at a spreadsheet that looks like a heartbeat, wondering if the tent in their parking lot will hold through the night.

Maybe they'll remember this:
The tent isn't chaos; it's courage under construction.
The doctrine isn't a rulebook; it's a rhythm.
And Belief—real Belief—isn't faith in yourself. It's faith that what you are building can one day stand without you, because it's a movement.

As the sun slid behind the Aiguille Rouge range, the light washed the Bosson glacier an iridescent pink and orange. The air tasted like metal and memory. I could see, in the distance, climbers returning—tiny figures, each carrying their own story of ascent and success and failure and return.

And I thought something quietly beautiful: I was one of them now. It made me profoundly happy.

I was a climber who'd built companies instead of ridgelines, who'd mapped doctrines instead of routes. Maybe the only legacy that mattered was leaving behind a map clear enough that others could keep climbing after you. I closed the notebook, tucked it into my jacket, and looked up at Mont Blanc and the Dome de Gouter one last time. The peak was already fading into dusk, the pink glow creeping slowly to darkness. The world would go on spinning, indifferent and beautiful. And somewhere—maybe in a tent in Fremont, or a clinic in Gothenburg, or an office in Cambridge—someone would pick up a tool, or a laser, or a line of code, and Act.

The loop would turn again. And again.

I finished my coffee. The church bell rang seven times.

EPILOGUE

Chamonix

Morning in Chamonix has a way of enlightening your heart. It's the truth of the sun first flooding the summits, then coating the valley below. The light comes in at an angle that makes the glaciers and Aiguilles look closer than they are and the day already feels shorter than you want it to be. Guides walk past the mountain shops the way surgeons walk down a corridor before an operation—calm, purposeful, already a few steps into the day, thinking, planning. If you listen closely, you can hear the clink of carabiners and ice screws swinging rhythmically into each other on a harness. You might pick up the hiss of skis over fresh snow, or the low murmur of people making plans that involve weather and consequence.

I come to Cham when I want to remember what belief feels like in the body. Not the TED Talk version. The real one. Lungs on fire, legs arguing and my mind running numbers while my eyes keep drifting to weather that suggests—politely at first—that you should turn around.

The mountains are corrective lenses for founders who confuse vision with motion. Up here there's no story, no pitch deck. There is only the line you choose, the step you take, and what the universe sends back in return. Every year that feedback is fatal for some. Too many of those who died were my friends. So many more were people I'll never know.

I've chased belief into the thin places of the planet, and it always leaves me grateful. A little wrecked. Fully awake. I've done it with my body and my mind. Some people call it insane. I call it a refusal to live this life halfway when I've been given the chance to live it fully.

Why mountain bike to the top of Europe's tallest peak, Mount Elbrus—especially the last fifty meters, blind in a full whiteout? Simple. To see if I could. Because once you commit, you either find the summit and then find your way back, or you disappear over the other side. Why start an RFID company that doesn't sell tags or readers or chips? Because I could see through the fog, across the Gap.

I've pedaled to the top of Africa on Mount Kilimanjaro and then scorched down. I've pointed my front wheel at the prayer flags of Everest Base Camp after an exhausting four day hike & bike from Lukla. I've crossed 350 miles of frozen Alaskan tundra during the Iditarod Invitational in February, four and a half days on a fat bike, sleeping ninety minutes a night while the air held steady at minus thirty-five. Celsius or Fahrenheit? At that temperature the numbers stop arguing. They agree, it's f*cking cold.

Those days stay with me. So do all-night bouts of testing and coding before a big launch. In the wild I remember what I carried. What I didn't. What I thought I needed and what actually saved me. I think about all the things that almost stopped me but didn't. Most of all, I remember who was there. Who shared the long quiet climbs and electrifying descents. Who shared the sleepless nights and failed demos.

Like every adventurer—and every founder—I always believed I'd come back to do it again.

The lesson the mountains teach—again and again, kindly when they can, harshly when they must—is the same lesson of this book. Belief is not a poster or a slogan. Belief is equipment. Belief is your partner. Belief is your training. Belief is knowing you will deliver even when you don't know how.

Belief is the downy insulation that keeps your core warm when the wind whips: the why that stops you from turning back at the first blast of resistance. It's the topo map you pull out when the sky closes, and every ridge looks like every other ridge: a shared view that turns panic into a path. And it's the helmet—unromantic, unfancy, unarguable—that keeps the inevitable falling rock from ending the entire trip: the guardrails that make bold action survivable.

Up high, Belief is specific. You don't "believe in success." Biking across glaciers on Elbrus with crevasses 50 meters deep I only believe in the next move: unclip, step, breathe, clip in, pedal. In companies, belief gets specific the same way: a creed you can say without looking at a slide; a Shared Belief Map on the wall for all to absorb and drive forward, not an idea in someone's head; a decision rule that lets the Single-Threaded Owner act today instead of asking permission tomorrow. You don't summit with theories. You summit with cadence.

On Elbrus, the summit morning started like a lot of decision meetings I've seen—everyone awake, nobody quite ready. The wind had opinions. The snow had texture. The night guarded its darkness. The route had a handful of good lines and a dozen bad ones that only looked good from far away. We did the same BOODA loop I've done all over the world: Believe, Observe, Orient, Decide, Act. Then we did it again a hundred times. The loop is not magic. The loop is discipline, anticipation and awareness.

On the Iditarod trail you learn to covet decisiveness. Fix the zipper now, not later. Eat when you're not hungry yet but can get the stove started easily. Change out of the sweaty layer before you're chilled to the bone. You are 300 miles from the nearest road and rescue by plane could take days. That's the founder's life in winter: the thousand tiny acts that keep the mission warm enough to continue. Your competitors will mistake that for luck. You'll know better. You didn't get lucky; you trained right, you packed right, you did the work.

If you've read this far, you've climbed with me—through a wire between towers, under a tent in Fremont, at a clinic in Gothenburg, in a courtroom in Israel, down a hallway at MIT, and in a top-secret server farm in Dulles. You've met a Finnish triathlete dragging societies across canyons of doubt, a CEO sleeping on concrete to push cars into being, and a team in Cambridge discovering that a map without a constitution is just wall art. You've seen the frigidity of Iridium and watched Friendster collapse into the Belief Glut and you've seen it harden into the rock-solid bridge that others can cross with Trulia. You know, now, that the job isn't to be right in theory; it's to be right *in time*. **You know that speed isn't frantic; it's frictionless and clean. You know that heroism is for headlines and hygiene is for companies that last.**

So here is what I want to leave with you from Chamonix, where the mountains make all speeches short.

First: thank you. You gave me your time and attention, which are the rarest currencies in the age of doom scrolling. You stayed for the stories, which is how

Belief travels. You were willing to see the doctrine not as another framework but as an operating rhythm you can run even when you're tired and almost out of fuel. I'm grateful—more than a sentence can carry—for founders like you who take ideas off a page and test them against the weather.

Second: a simple call to action. Don't wait for better conditions. Write your creed—one page, plain words. Build your Shared Belief Map and put it on a wall where no one can ignore it. Then Act.

Finally: remember what the summit is for. Your Creed is the summit. Your legacy is the view beyond it. The summit isn't the end of the climb; it's the first clear look at the next ridge and the people you want to guide there. Companies that endure don't end with their founders' schedules. They end when the creed runs out of believers. Your job is to make sure it doesn't—to build a factory of Belief that outlives your adrenaline, outlives your inbox, even outlives you.

From the valley, the Alps look indifferent. Up close, you realize they're generous—so long as you move with respect and decide with conviction. That's the bargain you get in business, too. The world won't guarantee you a path. There are risks. But, it will guarantee you feedback. You've got a doctrine now for what to do with that feedback—the BOODA Doctrine.

When the day starts in Chamonix, the sun slides around the Aiguille du Midi as if it's tracing a mystic pinkish-orange route for you. Alpinists shoulder their packs. An anxious client laughs with his guide, too loudly, in a fight to keep his nerves at bay. Someone else clicks into crampons with that small, satisfying sound of a plan becoming motion. It's not grand. It's not dramatic. It happens every day here. It's just the sound of people who chose to act.

Choose to act. Believe—explicitly. Observe—cleanly. Orient—together. Decide—with ownership. Act—decisively. Do it enough and your company will stop needing you to push; it will start pulling you forward. Do it long enough and one day you'll look up from your work, wherever your "Chamonix" is, and you'll recognize that your Creed is moving without you.

That's when you know you've built more than a business. You built a line others can follow. You built a view someone else will be in awe of. Philippe Petit stepped onto the wire alone. But you don't have to. The Founder's Creed is your team. The BOODA Doctrine is your balancing pole. The world is watching. The gap is waiting. Step onto the wire.

Thank you and Godspeed.

Patrick Sweeney

Chamonix, France | January 2026

ACKNOWLEDGMENTS

Writing a book is essentially the literary equivalent of a startup, except with fewer snacks and more existential dread. Since I'm not a fan of suffering in solitude, I recruited a small army of brilliant people to help. The result isn't just a book; it's a "treasure chest" of advice, though some might call it a highly organized collection of things I overheard smarter people saying. My goal is to help 1,000 of you build billion-dollar "unicorns." If you pull it off and use the BOODA Doctrine, please let me know because I want to give back to the start-up world that's given me so much.

The Hall of Fame (and Patience)

- **Thomas Lawaetz:** A massive thank you for letting me poke around in your life and livelihood for the sake of a "good story." You were my primary source of inspiration and a key reason I didn't abandon this project to become a professional goat herder. The **Nordic Health Group** saga is pure gold, and we're all lucky you're such an open book. It goes without saying every one of my readers and I will be looking forward to your Unicorn party!
- **The MedXit Mystery:** For those wondering, "MedXit" is actually

a Frankenstein's monster of two (okay, three) companies I've worked with recently. I stitched them together into one fictitious entity to better demonstrate the **BOODA Doctrine** without making the Table of Contents look like a phone book.

- **The Inner Circle:** Shout out to **Sami Inkinen** and **Pete Flint** for the great co-founder assists. Big thanks to the venture crews—**Rialto, Red Alpine, Patriot**, and **Milemark**—for the support.
- **Special Mentions:** Thanks to **Mike Troiano** for "the Glut" (he knows what he did) and my **YPO forum mates** for keeping me sane while my personal life tried to go off the rails.
- **YPO friends**: thank you to all the YPO members who gave advice, did an advance reading or voted for cover design. The organization needs some work, but the members across the globe are the most amazing group of humans I know and it has been life-changing to be a part of this family.
- **A big thank you to my family** who always are curious to what I'm doing and are never quite sure where I am or what I'm up to, but know I'm always here if they need me.
- During the eighteen months it took to write this book, I had the unforgettable experience of riding what I came to think of as the "OC Rollercoaster." It delivered some of the highest highs and a few of the hardest lows I've known. The journey changed me, taught me more than I expected, and left fingerprints on these pages. Like I learned my first time at Disney, some rides stay with you long after you step off them like you were destined to be on them, and if the tracks were ever rebuilt just a little differently, I suspect I'd still be curious or crazy enough to take another ride.

U

W

Y

Z

ABOUT THE AUTHOR

Patrick J. Sweeney II

Patrick J. Sweeney II is a 5x founder and CEO, *Wall Street Journal* Best-Selling Author, Venture Capitalist, and investor in over 75 startups. While his career is defined by high-stakes exits and global adventure, his understanding of belief began on the shores of Duncan Lake in Ossipee, New Hampshire.

Patrick's obsession with the "B" in the BOODA loop was sparked by his grandmother, Beatrice when he was just ten years old, as she rowed alongside him in an old aluminum john-boat during his first swim across the length of the lake. She planted the seed for an amazing life by being the first person to truly believe in him. That foundation was reinforced by his parents, Pat and Sandy, who instilled the unshakable creed that he could be whoever he wanted to be and do anything he wanted to do.

This early indoctrination in self-belief fueled a lifetime of "firsts," "onlys," and "what was I thinking:"

- **The Self-Made Maverick:** As the first person in his family to attend college, Patrick didn't just find a way—he built it, literally paying for his education by swinging a hammer. At the University of New Hampshire he discovered rowing and had the belief he could be world-class if he worked hard enough. The sport changed his life.
- **The Clinical Survivor:** He faced his own ultimate "Belief Gap" in an

oncology ward, surviving a rare form of Leukemia after being given only two weeks to live —a deadline he fortunately decided to treat as a "hypothesis" rather than a "core belief." He got a second chance to live an amazing life and he has made the most of that opportunity.

- **The Adventure Athlete:** He channeled his conviction into the global stage as an Olympic-level rower and elite athlete, finishing second in the US Olympic trials in the single scull and racing the World Cup for three years. After the Olympics and graduate school he eventually mountain biked to the summit of Mount Elbrus, Mount Kilimanjaro, Everest Base camp and many other peaks. He won the Race Across America cycling from California to Maryland along with three other founders and shares a similar decision making framework as Forest Gump.

- **The Tech Visionary:** After two back-breaking years of studying at the University of Virginia he founded and scaled industry-defining companies like ServerVault , ODIN , and dwinQ , presenting the BOODA Doctrine™ here for the first time—a system used in his own ventures and dozens of venture-backed successes over the last 25 years, and which he could have applied better at DaVinci 3.0 his last start-up.

- **The Eclectic Author:** *The Founder's Creed* is his fifth book and first one focused on entrepreneurs. His last book *Fear is Fuel: The Surprising Power to Help You Find Purpose, Passion and Performance* hit #5 on the WSJ Best-Seller List. He also produced a children's book called *Paddy Picks a Puppy* which helps pre-teens and teens learn about personality traits using the Enneagram system. His first book ever was published by John Wiley & Sons called *RFID for Dummies.* The second book was the CompTIA study guide for RFID certifications. He has a partial manuscript for a book called *Be Like Brutus* about his lifetime with dogs, keep an eye out for that one.

Today, Patrick splits time between Boston, Massachusetts and Chamonix, France. He remains a student of human potential, teaching founders that the "Belief Gap"—the space between your vision and where the world is today—is always crossable. *The Founder's Creed* is his gift to the next generation of entrepreneurs— a manual for turning personal conviction into a powerful, scalable asset.

Take the First Step

Are you living in a healthy Belief Gap or a dangerous Belief Glut? To diagnose your company's internal conviction and external validation, download the official Founder's Creed Workbook and complete the "Belief Gap Assessment" at www.thefounderscreed.com. Patrick and his team are also available for workshops and advisory services to venture backed companies and scale-up or pre-scale up startups.

Follow Patrick J. Sweeney II on Amazon author page and LinkedIn: